Just An Ordinary Man

Jim Parker

© 2009 Jim Parker
Just An Ordinary Man

ISBN 978-0-9561432-0-4

Published by Jim Parker at
Ordinary Man Publishing
Walstead Place
Great Walstead
Lindfield
Haywards Heath RH16 2QG

The right of Jim Parker to be identified as the author of this work has been asserted by him in accordance with the Copyright, Designs and Patents Act 1988.

All rights reserved. No part of this publication may be produced in any form or by any means – graphic, electronic or mechanical including photocopying, recording, taping or information storage and retrieval systems – without the prior permission, in writing, of the publisher.

A CIP catalogue record of this book
can be obtained from the British Library.

Book designed by Michael Walsh at
THE BETTER BOOK COMPANY
A division of
RPM Print & Design
2-3 Spur Road
Chichester
West Sussex
PO19 8PR

Contents

Acknowledgements........................... *overleaf*
Introduction.. i
1 Early years 1
2 Wartime and the R.A.F. 12
3 Immediate Post war life 43
4 Gatwick Airport 60
5 My Family 86
6 Life's Challenge 114
7 Anecdotes from my life
   - My teeth 124
   - Alec and Betty in St Mary's Bay .126
   - Driving 128
   - Food and Music 131
   - Dogs 134
8 Walstead Place and Friends...............139
9 Final thoughts 158

Illustrations

1 Air Craftsman Jim Parker 15
2 The Sunderland seaplane....................25
3 The Sunderland seaplane in the air 25
4 My War Medals .... after p 42
5 My Father's War Medals .... after p 87
6 Family Photographs............................94

Acknowledgements

I would like to thank Monica Eeson and Giada Sabbion for their help in the preparation of the manuscript and turning my numerous tape recordings into this book, which has been the realisation of a dream for me.

Introduction

It occurred to be to write my life story several years ago after a period of illness when I had been in a coma. I knew that I would write a story about my life called "Just An Ordinary Man". It is the only thing I remember about when I was ill. From that day about four years ago, I have been debating whether to do it because it would mean having to back so far in my memory. It has taken me four attempts and I think I have at last got it right. The idea for the book and the title just came to me when I was half conscious, and that is the whole truth. And that is what this book is based on – the truth.

Despite not being an educated man, I have led a full and interesting life and achieved much. It goes to show what Just An Ordinary Man can achieve. My eyesight is failing, so I did this by talking into a tape recorder and having it typed up for me, and bit by bit it has all come together. There have been so many trials and tribulations, so many life experiences and I welcome this wonderful opportunity and that I live to tell my story.

To my family, my wife, my daughter, my sons, grandchildren and great-grandchildren, I want you to know that you are the most important people in my life.

My family, I ask that you don't think for a moment that my loss of physical sight may have impaired my judgement. I assure you that my emotional vision has not failed me as I remain as sharp as ever.

I see, I hear and I appreciate,
I see, I hear and I give thanks,
I see, I hear, I forgive, but above all,
I see, I hear and I understand what is said and what goes unsaid.

Remember everyone, we have differences of opinion and interpret with our own yardsticks.

This is my story and I am happy to have had the opportunity to share it with you. I count my blessings and hope all who read my book will take the time to count and appreciate their blessings too for life can be a beast and prey on you when you're weakest. I suspect that perhaps some may not fully appreciate my story, but don't worry too much, for truly, wisdom does come with age.

I am sure that many will accuse me of being overly joyous in my views of people and that by now I've reached the age of diminished memory and distorted vision in terms of my judgement. I assure you that only my physical sight fails me and I remain as sharp as ever and vigilant of those around me.

To the people who made a difference in my life, thank you for being there for me. I would like to give thanks and pay my respects to my dear father-in-law and mother-in-law, Alfred and Sarah Gale who took me so warmly into their family.

I promised my mother that I would pray, and I believe Jesus really has taken care of me.

1

EARLY YEARS

I was born on 8th May 1920 in my Uncle Jack and Aunty Annie's laundry situated at 64 Amity Grove, Raynes Park. I think the laundry was called the Sunlight Laundry but I am not too sure about that. I was called Sunny Jim by my Aunt Annie because she said I smiled all the time and since then, the name Sunny Jim stuck.

When I was about five days old I was taken to the Evelina Hospital for Children in London and had to undergo an operation for a double rupture. My mother had told me that she had to hold a pad of camphorated oil over my nose and mouth whilst they carried out the operation.

Whilst the operation was carried out they also found that I had an enlarged appendix. They took it out and after a few days of being put into recovery, the nurses weren't happy with my progress. They took blood tests and when the results came in, I had anaemia and general debility. I don't know what general debility means these days, but can only imagine that it was weakness. When I was discharged from hospital, my mother had to take me to the doctor every fortnight in Raynes Park.

I have distinct and fond memories of my childhood. One was when I was between the age of three and four years old, my mother picked me up and said to me, "Sunny Jim, I'm putting you in the pram out of the way." She put me into this huge well-padded pram with very, very good suspension. I used to be wheeled up and down the kerb when mother took me out and such was the comfort that I didn't even feel the bumps. The pram my mother pushed me in was similar to those used by the nannies who walked babies in the Royal Parks in London. The nannies would walk in twos and threes in their black and white uniforms, chatting away to one another.

In my pram, I was fortunate to have company. I would be put into the pram and at the other end to me were my two cousins Ivy and Louise. They were roughly about my age. I remember how my cousins and I would stretch our arms toward each other and reach out to make contact, but the pram was so huge and we were so little, it was impossible for our fingers to touch, so we'd just content ourselves in our baby language. Strange as it may seem, I find that when I concentrate, even though I'm at the age of 88, I can still hear the sound of our small voices in my mind, and I can still visualise the reaching out to each other with fair clarity.

I was very close to my mother and I always remember the deep affection she expressed when she talked to me. Many fond memories flow when I sit back and think about my mother, like the time she revealed something I hold dear to my heart till today. It was on my fourth birthday and she had crouched down to be at eye level with me. She took my two tiny hands into hers. The affection in her own eyes was immense – I knew she loved me dearly and that what she was about to tell me was something very, very important.

She said to me, "Jimmy, you're four years old today and I want to tell you about someone else beside me or your dad that will always take great care of you. I want to tell you about Jesus and how important it is to pray to him every day." I don't remember all the detail, but I do remember how precious it seemed to my mother that I understood the importance of having Jesus in my heart and praying to him everyday.

With the understanding of a four year old which I equate to 'total confusion' of who this Jesus was, but nevertheless decidedly trustful of my mother's words of wisdom, I listened with intent. Her eyes were soft and compassionate, her voice warm and sincere. I stood there absorbing and experiencing this great atmosphere of love. Both my little hands still wrapped in hers, she continued to explain Jesus. I remained silent but strongly aware of the importance of the message she was revealing. There was an indescribable passion for me in this message.

We understood each other and with that, I put my arms around her and thanked her for this entrusted information of the Jesus who would look out for me. Mother touched my face lightly with emphasised affection then placed her hand upon my head and said, "God Bless You My Child." I trusted my mother and from that day on, I prayed to Jesus and I am thankful that I listened to her for although at the age of four I can admittedly say I didn't quite understand the words, I can testify to the unforgettable ambience my mother created, sufficiently transparent for four year old me to have got the message of Jesus. Today I can stand up and count the blessing I received because I prayed to Jesus everyday and I still do so now.

My sister was eight months old at the time my mother told me about Jesus and perhaps important timing too. Mother breastfed my sister, so she had been unable to give me much attention. Fortunately I never ever felt neglected because my dad was as wonderful and as affectionate as my mother and he used to take over the responsibility of looking after me when mother nursed and fed my sister. Dad would put me on his lap, sing and teach me old war songs. He was a wonderful dad and of course there was Jesus too looking out for me.

When I was five years old, we moved into a flat in Wimbledon at 13a Cowper Road. Our flat was upstairs and had a wrought iron staircase that led down to our side of the garden. The other side of the garden belonged to the downstairs flat, number 13 occupied by Mr & Mrs Knott. I was not allowed to go down to play in the garden because the iron staircase leading to the garden was very dangerous and my mother was afraid I would fall down and hurt myself.

We were very, very poor at the time of moving into 13a Cowper Road, Wimbledon and my parents had no money to buy food. I remember that at approximately 12 o'clock each day, we'd all go down to the middle of Cowper Road to wait for the soup kitchen to come around. The soup kitchen was a horse and cart with an urn on the back containing the soup. Many families were in our same predicament and had to line up for food. They were hard times back in those days and jobs were difficult to come by.

We had a coal cellar downstairs next to Mrs Knott and the coalman would come round once a week with his horse and cart. Wimbledon Hill was so steep that he had to ride the horse and he had to have a relief horse to help draw the cart up the hill carrying the heavy load of coke and coal. We would order 50 kilos of coal or coke. The coke served a double purpose. My mother would light a coke fire and would also heat the iron to do the family ironing. We couldn't use the coal as it would dirty the clothes.

This was the only form of heating and my father used to have to find wood to chop into sticks and use rolls of paper crumpled up into balls, placed under the sticks with the coke on top in order to light the fire. Each day the remains of the grate had to be cleaned in preparation for a fresh fire. My father used to carry up a coal scuttle of coal or coke for every day.

My dad would go out each day and look for

work and eventually he was lucky enough to find temporary work with Wimbledon Borough Council as a navvy. His job was to pick and shovel the roads all around Wimbledon and each night he'd come home with aches and pains from the hard labour of his job. He never complained because he knew if you didn't work, you didn't get an income and he was grateful to have a job even though it was only temporary and broke his back. Dad was a hard-working man and slowly the money trickled in and my mother was able to go to the shops to buy a few items that she previously couldn't have afforded.

Commitment and hard work paid off, as after the three weeks of temporary work with Wimbledon Borough council my dad was offered permanent work. It wasn't too long after when he was promoted to become what was called a 'ganger man' which in today's terms would translate to a foreman.

During this time, our family were becoming more prosperous and we didn't need the soup kitchens. We were fortunate enough to have been allocated an allotment where we were able to grow all the fruit and vegetables possible for the season. Sadly we had to throw away fruit and vegetables that became soft as we didn't have fridges back them to keep them fresh. As I mentioned before, dad was a very hard-working man and apart from his permanent job at the Council and the upkeep of the allotment, he also worked part-time for the

Lawn Tennis Association in Wimbledon. There he was responsible for looking after the men's toilets. He met with all the famous tennis players during the Wimbledon tournament and said how marvellous and kind they all were. It was the fortnight of every year he thoroughly enjoyed.

As things started looking up for dad, the spare cash he earned meant he could go to the pub on a Sunday to enjoy his two pints of beer. He was a disciplined man and would never drink more than his two pints, then, on his way home he would stop at the little stall near the pub and buy some cockles, winkles, shrimps and mussels and bring them home for our lunch which we had with some bread and butter. My sister and I used to get the winkles out with a pin. Mother couldn't stand watching us and would look away as my sister and I carefully extracted our winkles with a pin onto our plates. When we had finished, only then would mother start to eat her lunch. Dad on the other hand was not fussy and would eat anything!

I didn't have a normal childhood in terms of hopscotch, skip and jump. I was too frail and weak to be allowed to go to school or play outside with anyone. My mother kept me home from school until I was twelve years old. I was so weak; I couldn't even bounce a tennis ball. I would sit upstairs in my front room and watch the children down below playing all sorts of games, laughing and joking. How I wished to join in the fun, but my mother was very protective and explained that she was afraid that I would get hurt and had to keep me home from school and play on doctor's orders. I never argued with her as I knew she knew better than I did. Despite my fragile disposition physically, the dedicated love and attention from my parents built inner strength and shaped my determination for things to come.

My early years were closely monitored and every Monday morning, mother took me to the Doctor in Wimbledon. His name was Dr Spears, a wonderful old Doctor. There was no pharmacist in those days, and doctors had to keep the medicines in their surgery. Wealthy doctors were determined by the amount of medicines they kept and poor doctors were determined by the amount of medicines they didn't have. Dr Spears had a good selection of medicines, so I guess he was considered a wealthy doctor. I remember little about the medicines he administered, but one thing I clearly remember was cod liver oil and malt, I loved it. In fact, when I got the chance, I'd open the pot and take a crafty spoonful every now and again.

Another favourite time from my early years was the walk home from Dr Spears' surgery. On the way home, every Monday morning, we would go into a toy shop and my mother would let me look in the glass cabinet filled with toy soldiers. These were made of lead and their arms and legs moved and they had proper boots on. I collected them for five years and think I had about 250 eventually when I left school. I used to have all sorts of soldiers, from various regiments, horses, cannons. The canons had a little lever which if you pulled it back about a quarter of an inch with a matchstick and let the lever go, it would shoot the matchstick across about 12 inches. I pretended to fire and then laid down the little soldier and said he was dead. They were happy days.

At the age of twelve, I approached my mother and told her that I wanted to go to school. She agreed and the following Monday she accompanied me to school for my first time. I couldn't read or write, so I was put into a class with five year olds, but the desks and chairs were too small for me to sit at. The teacher didn't think it was a good idea to keep me in the class of five year olds and suggested that I be moved to my own group age. My inability to read and write didn't stop me from the desire to learn and the one subject that really interested me was chemistry.

At this time, I used to go out with four or five boys from Cowper Road down to somewhere near to Colliers Wood underground station. On the bend on every Derby Day we used to go with a lot of other boys from Wimbledon onto a corner and wait for the coaches and caravans returning from Epsom. We'd call out "Throw out your mouldies Mister" and we used to get dozens of coins thrown out of the window. This happened every year.

I eventually left school at the age of fourteen

and was fortunate enough to find work immediately with a company called Fosters Engineering Company located on the old Morden Road. I was put in the stores and my job was to sweep up and keep the place tidy. I had to familiarise myself with all the equipment and make sure that any odd pieces not used on the factory floor were put away.

I worked hard and was able to save up enough to buy myself a lovely emerald green BSA lightweight cycle. It was a fixed wheel racing club cycle and without brakes. One day my supervisor Roy Collins whom I had become very friendly with asked me if I was interested in joining a road racing club with him. Roy Collins was considerably older than me and was a knowledgeable man. Together we joined the Old Portlians Cycling Club on the old Upper Norwood Road. I participated in the 100 mile races which were routed from London to Brighton. I took part in many. One very hot summer's day on one of my rides, I had pushed so hard in my effort to reach the destination in Brighton that the sweat on my face had crystallised and turned to a very fine powder-like salt. I hadn't been aware of my salty face; it was pointed out to me by some of the lads I rode with.

The fastest time I achieved riding for Old Portlians, was four hours forty-five minutes to cover 100 miles non-stop. That was nothing like a record, but considering my fragile frame, it was most certainly was a record for me since I had been so weak for the first twelve years of my life, and now here I was at last with the strength to ride in a one hundred mile marathon. My routine before setting off on the London/Brighton one hundred mile ride was to leave home with two raw eggs. Before the start of the race, I would break the two eggs and chuck them down my throat. They slipped down so quickly you didn't have time to taste them. I would swear by that to give me energy and this became my ritual each time I participated in a race. My training schedule was to go for a row on the River Thames from Kingston to Hampton Court and back every week with Roy, using a double rowing boat which was reserved for us by an owner at a staging point every Saturday.

Roy and I were invited to the Norwood Paragon Club (not far away from the Old Portlians) and race there. We accepted the invitation and went to ride for the Paragon Club, one of the most famous cycle racing clubs in the world. I met two people called Bill Poole and Ken Mackintosh. Bill Poole was a small man and Ken Mackintosh was very heavy-set man. They were the world and Olympic champions for tandem riding from 1934 to 1939. They were two smashing men and I will never forget them because they had taken me under their wing and helped me tremendously with everything.

2

WARTIME AND THE RAF

In 1939, just before my birthday on the 8th May, there was murmur and talk of war. I sat down to consider what I could do as I didn't want to be called up to the army to do any old job. I decided that I would sign on for the Air Force. I discussed this with a few friends and they all seemed concerned about my RAF consideration insisting that I would fail the medical. They also felt that my lack of education would hinder my chances to be considered for the Air Force. I chose to ignore the negativity about my circumstance and asked my friend Roy Collins to help me write a letter to the Air Ministry to request an application form to join the RAF.

Roy wrote the letter for me and I remember being nervous about how I would have to respond when the form eventually arrived. A few days later, the form arrived and it was a lot simpler than expected. All I had to do was complete twelve general knowledge questions. I didn't know the answers to any of the questions but that didn't deter me. I randomly marked twelve boxes as was required and Roy sent the form back for me. Not long after, I received an invitation to attend the RAF Enrolment Centre in London. I knew that I would have to leave secretly so as not cause my parents any concern, so the morning of the interview, I packed my saddlebag as if I was going to work. The RAF letter had instructed that I bring my shaving kit and underclothes. I didn't understand why at the time, but I soon learned when I got there.

I arrived at the Air Ministry Centre and I counted approximately forty recruits lining up to join. They seemed roughly my age and some a bit older, some tall, some short. We filed in one by one and the first thing to happen was the medical examination. We were told to strip to the waist and stand in a row. Then we were ordered to drop our pants and we all stood with nothing on. The medical officer examined every one of us and even used a torch. He seemed to take ages, especially when he got to me. I don't know if it was because I was thin or what, but he spent a lot of time with me. I held my breath wondering if I would get through.

Finally the examination ended and three men were rejected and the other thirty-seven were commissioned to the room next door to get uniforms and equipment. I was one of the thirty-seven. We were each given two sets of uniforms with a Glengarry hat and a special ceremonial cap with a peak and white ceremonial belt which had to be blancoed every time we wore it. We were also given boots which we had to keep spotlessly clean. We used our spit and polish to keep our boots clean and shiny. After collecting what we required, we were told to get into a lorry and whilst waiting, we all swapped uniforms as some of us had trousers too long or short, jackets too big or too small. Some wouldn't even button up; we all tried our best to fit one another out. All 37 of us were kitted out with the right sizes.

The lorry eventually moved off and after a very long ride, we stopped at 9.00 pm in Blackpool, but nowhere near the seafront. We were dropped off in an unused playground.

So there I was at 9.00 pm at night, in Blackpool, my parents and sister would have been waiting for me to arrive home after work at about 5.30 pm. I thought whatever am I going to do? I felt very guilty that they would be worrying about me but at the same time I felt very satisfied because I had got into the RAF when everyone else had thought I wouldn't. (See photograph opposite of the newly recruited Air Craftsman Parker.)

I decided to send my mother a telegram which read, "Dear Mum, I've joined up, I'm in Blackpool and I'm going to wait to be posted from Blackpool in about a month's time as I'm in the RAF." She didn't like this one bit, as when I went back on my first leave, she had completely emptied my bedroom, got rid of my bed, wardrobe etc and the only things she didn't get rid of was my Meccano set, my Hornby railway, my soldiers and my fort – everything else had gone. On my first leave, I had to go and sleep at my Aunty and Uncle's at the laundry.

Air Craftsman Jim Parker

After two days my mother and father bought me a bed and wardrobe and told me to come back home and they forgave me.

I had felt awful about the hurt I caused my mother when I had signed up, but I felt it was a decision well thought through given that I didn't want to be called up. As a volunteer, I had a say in what I wanted to be trained in. I trained as a SEW, a Safety Equipment Worker in charge of the maintenance and repair of parachutes and dinghies, although that trade didn't come for a long while.

After reaching Blackpool, we were then told we were going on a train. The trains had no connecting carriages, all single carriages. The trains were very long and absolutely packed. We were a group of twelve recently signed up raw recruits, ordered to meet at the station and get onto the train. None of us knew each other or each other's names. We were kitted out with our rifles, bayonets, ammunition, ground sheets, sleeping blankets and various other bits and pieces that made up a very heavy load on our backpacks.

We mounted the train, but each designated to different carriages so we were in effect split up, but all headed for the same destination. The train pulled off and the journey seemed to have no end, stopping at various stations to discharge or pick up passengers. It was only during the stops that a NAAFI trolley came along the platform selling cups of tea, cakes, biscuits and sandwiches, just basics and certainly not beer, which I am sure many would have appreciated.

We would have to lean out of the window or open the door to buy from the NAAFI trolley. The journey was long and tedious and we had no idea where we were being posted or when we'd reach our destination. Many folk got on and off, but we were instructed to stay on. In total I calculated forty-eight hours, when we eventually stopped in Aberdeen and were told to dismount.

It was cold and damp and we were exhausted. All twelve recruits were reunited and ordered to get onto a boat. I was perplexed and I noted that so were the others. I thought we had joined the Air Force, so why then were we getting onto a boat? No one was brave enough to ask, so we picked up our backpacks and all got onto the boat knowing full well that this was to be yet another long drawn out journey.

Twenty-four hours later, the boat eventually docked at Lerwick, the capital of the Shetland Isles. We looked around and saw snow-capped hills and mountains and lots of sheep. No houses, or farmsteads, just sheep, hills and mountains. We stood there mystified when we were approached by a commander in charge who then told us to get into a coach. There were other people on it besides us. We arrived at a place called Sullom Voe, a very big voe in the middle of the Shetland Isles. When we dismounted, we seemed to be the only people to leave the coach.

So there we stood, in the midst of fog and gloom on the bank of Sullom Voe. Had they dropped us off at the edge of the world and forgotten about us? No one spoke; our surroundings beckoned silence and attention, although you could hear the rubbing of hands of the individuals who tried to keep warm. We stood listlessly beside our heavy backpacks, each recruit wearing his own expression of question and bewilderment.

I was sure they had made a mistake; there was no one or nothing around us that indicated that we were going anywhere. I wrestled with the idea in my head as I gazed as far into the distance as I could see. I too shuffled about to keep warm aware of the uncomfortable silence and biting cold, when suddenly the sound of a motorboat could be heard approaching.

The boat pulled up beside us and we were told to board. The silence between individuals continued as we lifted ourselves and our heavy kits into the speed boat. We sat there for quite a distance as the boat cruised toward a ship called SS (Steam Ship) *Manila*.

Boarding the SS *Manila* was quite an ordeal. It had a rope ladder hanging down the side. The steps were in wood, about 4 inches wide, just about enough to get the front part of your foot secured, in order to climb up. We had to negotiate ourselves up this wobbly, rope wooden stepladder with our backpacks on. At this stage I remember feeling a sudden surge of energy despite my exhaustion as we all climbed up with only a four-step distance between us. I was third from the top and had no intention of falling off the rope ladder. I can gladly report that there were no casualties and that we all managed to board safely. As we reached the top, we were helped on board by Alaskan sailors.

The captain briefed us about the ship and said that the SS *Manila* was brought back into service at the beginning of the war in 1939. It was crewed by 120 Alaskan sailors who were also responsible for loading the bombs and torpedoes onto the Sunderland flying boats. He told us that the ship weighed 8000 tons when fully loaded. We listened and captain rattled on, but one thing for sure, no one understood the concept of 8000 tons; that information was definitely beyond our young minds.

The induction ended with the twelve of us being split up into three groups. Group one was responsible for taking messages between the captain and other parts of the ship. Group two was commissioned to carry out odd jobs and group three was selected to carry out sentry duty, which is the group I belonged to.

We were eventually accompanied to our cabins. By now, nothing shocked us. Each moment from the time we left London presented diverse challenges. Experience after experience showed that you had to be prepared to accept and endure whatever was thrown at you, after all; this was wartime.

Our cabin was a small area with fifteen

hammocks slung about two feet below the rafters. In it there was a table and some chairs where we would eat our meals. The living conditions were deplorable, but that is what we had to put up with. We were told that due to such unpleasant living quarters we would only be required to serve on the ship for six months. Six months was still a stretch, but somehow the information presented a light form of relief.

We eventually settled in, but I must emphasise that the cabin was dreadful. We had to put up with the discomfort of the hammocks as well of the constant noise caused by the dozens of rats that lived two feet above us in the rafters, gnawing away at the ropes that held up the hammocks. Our first night there was hell, but we were so beat, we managed to finally get to sleep. It took some getting used to, but the annoying little beast feasts were by comparison insignificant against the many challenges I imagined we would endure in the future.

It was the beginning of the war in September 1939 when suddenly we heard a noise. The bomber plane overhead dropped a bomb. I suspect it was aimed for the ship, but it was dropped a mile away from us in the hills. A great plume of smoke went up on the sky.

There were four of us off duty from our shifts. This was about the third day that we'd been on the ship when the bomb was dropped. Still not acquainted with each other by name or sort, we got chatting about the incident. We were all curious and eager to assess the damage caused by the bomb, so we asked the Captain if he'd allow us permission to use the motor boat to go up to the hill. The Captain agreed, so we set off with the obvious trepidation and curiosity of four naïve youths. I am sure the Captain had permitted the adventure with a measured degree of regard. He knew the importance of this trip to us.

We followed the direction of the smoke and negotiated where it had fallen. When we eventually got over there, we found an area of about four – five square yards where there were six dead rabbits. They weren't blown to pieces; it had been the shock that killed them. There was one little rabbit which we thought was still alive. We picked it up and stroked it till it responded. It was probably just dazed and after resuscitating it, we let it hop off.

We were all shocked at the devastation. We had asked to be out there to witness the damage, and now emotionally feeling the impact. The reality was deeply upsetting. We sat down and considered what had happened. Apart from the poor rabbits strewn across the field and the large crater in the hill, we all knew too well that this bomb missed its target by a mile. We had had a lucky escape.

The mood was sombre as reality of what could have been sunk in. Then suddenly out of the blue one of the lads piped out. "I know, let's write a song." We looked at him amused; he had broken the sombre mood we'd all assumed.

"We can't write a song," exclaimed one of the other lads.

"Of course we can, I'll write the music, hum it and you lot write the words, I have a pencil and paper in my pocket." We weren't convinced, but soon, he started to hum a tune. It was a simple melody and since I used to play the harmonica, I quickly picked up the rhythm. The words started to come to me and I scribbled them on the small piece of paper. So there we were, four recruits sitting on a bomb-blasted hill composing a sing-song. One humming the tune, two tapping to the beat, and me scribbling away.

> Run rabbit, run rabbit, run, run, run,
> Run rabbit, run rabbit, run, run, run,
> Please Mr Farmer get your gun, gun, gun,
> Run rabbit, run rabbit, run, run, run,
>
> Run rabbit, run rabbit, run, run, run,
> Run rabbit, run rabbit, run, run, run,
> Please Mr Farmer shoot your gun, gun, gun,
> Run rabbit, run rabbit, run, run, run,
>
> Run rabbit, run rabbit, run, run, run,
> Run rabbit, run rabbit, run, run, run,
> Bang, bang, bang went the farmer's gun,
> Run rabbit, run rabbit, run, run, run,
>
> Run rabbit, run rabbit, run, run, run,
> Run rabbit, run rabbit, run, run, run,

We'll get by without our rabbit pie,
Run rabbit, run rabbit, run, run, run.

It was a dark and dismal day; no sun and the wind was blowing. I sat on the bank with my feet dangling down toward the water contemplating. I was thinking about the poor rabbits. Seeing them scattered across the field had really upset me. It would have been a far better death had they been shot rather than suffer the consequences of a bomb blast.

We left the hill and returned to the ship feeling slightly better with the distraction of the sing-along song that we'd composed. When we got back to the ship I got out my harmonica and played it back to the boys. The song became so popular; all the crew on the ship sang or hummed it. It was quite incredible how infectious the melody had become.

The SS *Manila* was a very depressing environment so I would be allowed to leave the ship every Saturday to catch a little bus that travelled once a day from Sullom Voe to Lerwick Village. The bus would depart from Sullom Voe at 10.00 am then return at 4.00 pm in the afternoon. I'd go to Lerwick each Saturday to treat myself to lunch, and then I'd stand in the main shopping square and play my harmonica. A crowd would gather around me and enjoy listening to me play. I played all sorts of tunes and, of course, the famous little sing-song that myself and the other crew had created 'Run Rabbit, Run Rabbit, Run, Run, Run'.

The local residents on this Shetland Island became accustomed to my Saturday musical treats and I'd even get them to sing 'Run Rabbit, Run'. I think that this is how the little song might have spread its wings and gained its popularity eventually making its way to the agents of Flanagan and Allen.

My experiences on the ship were destined to stay with me forever, like when our ship was surrounded by Sunderland aircraft. (photographs on opposite page.) These were flying boats that only landed on water. There were seven in a squadron and these boats were positioned all around our ship. Our job was to support the special equipment needed for these aircraft. They used to fly escort ship convoys from Scapa Flow to the South Atlantic. We were always escorted by the Royal Navy – and my goodness they were great. HMS *Belfast*, HMS *London*, HMS *Coventry*, HMS *Glasgow*. I think HMS *Coventry* may have been a cruiser on a large destroyer, but they never left us. My goodness, when they opened their guns up on an aircraft that tried to bomb us, you would really know – God bless the navy.

We were often invited on board other ships to meet and socialise with other crew members. We couldn't invite others to our ship as it was too dirty and cramped. When we went on board other ships, they would arrange a small coach load of local girls to go on board and there would be

The Sunderland afloat ...

and in the air

singing, laughter and dance. I always took my harmonica with me and we would sing the song we composed on the bomb-blasted hill, 'Run Rabbit, Run'.

The song grew from strength to strength and ship to ship. It had become so popular that the Captain called me up to say that he had received a message over the radio from the agent of Flanagan and Allan asking if they could use the song in some of their opening numbers. I was nineteen at the time, had never heard of Flanagan and Allan, and knew nothing of copyrights, so I agreed for them to use the song. Years later, I heard the song being used in the popular *Dad's Army* show except that the words were different to the original words I had composed. I have since bought a CD with a selection of Flanagan and Allen songs. They start the CD with 'Run Rabbit, Run'. They said, when they asked to use it, that they would use it as their opening number, which is what they have done.

Time passed and it was time for some of us to go on leave. We had to draw lots for who would be the first to take leave. I was the lucky one on the first draw and made my way home. I was granted eleven days leave, three to travel and seven official leave days. The journey home was equally as awful as the journey to the ship when we first travelled.

I arrived home and one of the first people I met up with was my good old friend Roy. We would go to the cinema or cycling depending on the weather. One night, we were walking down the road. The searchlights were shining and sirens going in the background, giving people air raid warnings. Every household had blacked out windows and no one was allowed to light a match or shine a torch. As we walked along the road, I nudged Roy and said, "I can hear some girls ahead of us, I reckon I'll go and have a chat with them." Roy eyed me with uncertainty, and then told me that he wasn't keen on the idea, so he crossed the road to walk on the other side. I hurried along and caught up with the girls and got chatting to them.

We walked along for quite a distance, enough time for me to learn that the young lady who walked beside me was called Dorothy and the other young lady on the far end of Dorothy was her friend Connie. By this time, Roy had craftily crossed the road and was walking and chatting away to Connie. Our acquaintance was just warming up when suddenly Dorothy exclaimed, "this is where we live."

She smiled reservedly and I looked up to notice her father looming above at the porch. I smiled back and declared that we were making sure the girls got home safely as the air raid warning was going. He bid me good evening and went into the house. I hurriedly asked Dorothy if she would be willing to write to me and me to her, when I got back to my ship. She agreed and this pleased me greatly for I had found a pen pal.

I returned to duty on the ship, but it was some weeks before I received any mail. During the war, mail didn't get priority and all the convoys coming out from Britain to our route on the Shetland Isles took a long time arriving. Consequently I got several letters together and when I next received mail there were about six letters. It was difficult to tell which order they arrived as letters were not allowed to be dated for security reasons. I wrote back and hoped Dorothy would understand my writing as it wasn't as good as hers.

Finally, six months had gone by and we were being replaced by twelve different men posted in for us to go home on leave. Eleven men had their names called out and for some unknown reason; I was the only one not granted leave. As was the norm, I did not question the decision and continued to work on the ship writing to Dorothy during my breaks. In one of my letters I had asked if we could arrange to meet up when I was next granted leave.

The next six months passed and I made my way home. I was excited about this leave, as I had arranged to meet up with Dorothy at the bus stop on the corner of Campbell Road, West Croydon where there was a big church. I dismounted the bus and saw a young lady standing across from my bus stop. I looked over and waved assuming that it was Dorothy. I remember thinking how attractive she was considering I had met her in the blackout and wondered if she would think the same about me! She walked toward me. "Hello, are you Jim"?

"Yes, I'm Jim," I said.

"Was your journey okay? I imagine you're very tired," she politely enquired.

We walked up the road to 25 Campbell Road. I was impressed to see this lovely three-storey house with six steps up to the front door and lovely pillars on either side. I entered the house and was confronted by the beautiful sound of very excited sweet voices of many girls exclaiming, "It's Jim, he's arrived, hurry, hurry, ssssshhhooo."

When I got inside, I counted five young ladies, chatting excitedly, giggling as girls do. I wondered what I had let myself in for! There was a lot of excited but hushed tones of laughter and exchange of words. Among the confusion, I quickly learned that four of the girls were Dorothy's sisters and the other girl, Beattie, was from next door, and had come in to see what I looked like. How wonderful it felt, this moment of stardom, being surrounded by a gathering of beautiful young ladies. The giggling simmered down and one of the ladies announced, "I'm Dorothy!"

I guess at that moment I looked confused, but I did gesture toward Dorothy approvingly and stepped forward to greet her warmly. As I did so, I enquired teasingly, "If you're Dorothy who met me at the bus stop? You all look so alike."

"Violet met you," Dorothy smiled back her reply.

In a proud gentlemanly fashion, I took Dorothy's hand, kissed it lightly and said, "Lovely to see you again Dorothy and thank you for agreeing to meet with me!"

From that day forth, Dorothy and I courted. We went out often to watch shows. Our favourite was the Davis Centre in Croydon where we used to watch the organ come up out of the ground playing beautiful songs before the film started. We also went to Wimbledon theatre to see the marvellous pantomimes.

I continued my service on the boat and I remember another time when our group of twelve were schedule to take leave, eleven men were granted leave and I wasn't on the list. This time I remained on the boat for eighteen months. As I mentioned before, living conditions on the boat were abominable. This time, I approached the Captain and requested compassionate leave to go and see my MP.

I returned home to see my local MP in Wimbledon; I think his name was Vernon Bartlett. I met with him at his office. When he saw me he immediately exclaimed how unusual it was to see an RAF man in his office. He went on to say what a coincidence he thought our meeting was, as he always wondered who the RAF men were on the ship I worked.

He informed me that he was present in the House of Commons at the time of Churchill's decision about the SS *Manila* and that Churchill spoke about the old boat being out of service for many years and as no good to anybody. Churchill had however, wanted to make use of the old ship and to get the SS *Manila* to the Shetland Isles, load her up with ammunition to supply a squadron of aircraft and flying boats, useful to back up the RAF bomber command, thus allowing aircraft to slip in and out whenever they wanted. In effect therefore, the SS *Manila* could serve a purpose only in support of the squadron of aircraft. The underlying tone of his decision was that of winning the war at all costs. In fact, Churchill went as far as suggesting that twelve raw recruits be posted onto the SS *Manila* and openly gave no value to their well being or whether or not they survived – I was one of the twelve. It had been clear from the outset that Churchill valued victory over life and he had openly admitted that he wasn't bothered if boat or recruits were lost at war.

"So you're one on the lads on that boat?" asked my MP, "What is it I can do for you then?"

I explained my situation of how I had been on the boat for eighteen months and had not been granted leave. I asked if he could investigate and assist me to obtain an alternative posting. "I'll do my damn best to get you off that boat," he assured me and with that, we shook hands and I left his office.

I returned to duty on SS *Manila* and by the time I got back, two twenty-four hour journeys plus a boat ride back, I was called in by the Captain.

"Mr Parker, you've got a posting to Croydon. Do you know Croydon?" he enquired. "Do I know Croydon?" I exclaimed with unreserved excitement. "Why, it's where my girlfriend lives!" I replied.

I arrived at Croydon Aerodrome. This was where we had to report to daily and from there, taken to Biggin Hill. There were only a few of us. I was housed in a four-bedroomed house in Wallington Road as there was no accommodation available at Croydon Airport. We were housed next to Polish pilots who risked coming over to the UK after Germany invaded Poland. These were brave men determined to help us win the war. I really admired and liked them and we became very friendly with these men.

Whilst I was part of the RAF, I had applied to learn a trade. One of my postings had been to RAF Melksham training centre for all trades. Pilots and engineers were trained in Cranwell. The RAF Melksham was commanded by a wing commander who was responsible for all training officers. At the end of my four-week training, I was approached by the wing commander. He was considered very high rank and it used to be an honour if he came to speak to you. He wanted me to join the S.E.W. unit (Safety Equipment Worker.)

"AC Parker, I think you are a born leader of men and women. You have passed this course with honours; therefore, I'm going to have you promoted right away to corporal. You've got outstanding abilities for learning so I congratulate you. I hope you go very far."

I saluted him. "Thank you, sir." He saluted me, and then shook my hand vigorously.

My posting to Croydon made it easy for me to visit Dorothy and her family. I visited often and we would sit for hours with Dorothy's parents and sisters discussing various topics, but as you imagine, war was the primary topic at the time. During the war, our courting was generally restricted to chats in the living room or the kitchen. When the air-raid siren went off, we would all have to rush to the shelter which was built underground in the garden. Every household had one of these shelters and we'd sometime spend hours down there in the cold and damp. We'd all be huddled up in this small area waiting for the safety signal to go off. I became very close to Dorothy and I eventually asked for her hand in marriage. I had to ask her dad and I can confirm that he seemed happy for me to wed his daughter.

The wedding date was set for 9th May 1942. We married in a lovely old church located at the back of Mayday hospital in Croydon. The church was picturesque with beautiful rambling roses all around the door. I think Dorothy and my parents had paid for the wedding, as I did not have much money. It was a wonderful wedding with quite a lot of family and friends, particularly from Dorothy's side. I had invited six of my very close friends from the RAF. One of the guys I invited played the drums at my wedding. Dorothy and I sang 'Apple Blossom Time' and were hugely applauded by our guests despite singing so softly. I remember thinking we weren't that good, but I guess as bride and groom you're bound to be made to feel special, and our guests certainly honoured that sentiment on our behalf.

On 12th March 1943, our first child was born. A beautiful bouncing baby girl we called Valerie Ann. From day one, Valerie Ann was destined to be my little princess and I adored her. Valerie was not very old when I was posted to Africa.

Nobody knew that I had received a secret message from the Air Ministry to take fourteen other men plus myself to Africa. I was under oath not to disclose my mission, not even to the men whom I was commissioned to accompany.

I secretly prepared my kitbag and took it downstairs. We lived in a top-floor flat at the time. Dorothy never missed a trick and must have sensed that I might have been called away on duty. I was downstairs arranging my kit and I gazed up to see Dorothy at the top of the stairs watching me. She had Valerie Ann wrapped in typical Welsh fashion. Back in those days, babies were wrapped in a shawl in a very protective manner. Their arms and heads would be wrapped and tucked in with only their wee faces showing.

Still fiddling with my kit, lifting and tugging at it to try to position it at the bottom of this narrow stairway, it's sheer weight required concerted effort to negotiate some form of balance and stability as I lifted it in to position up against the wall. Then, suddenly, I saw Dorothy come head first down the stairs, tumbling from one step after the other screaming out. Valerie Ann was completely silent as she tumbled down the stairs with Dorothy. With my heart in my mouth and in an instant, rid of the kit, I rushed to Dorothy and Valerie's aid.

It had all happened in a flash, I could do little till they landed at the bottom of the narrow stairway, suddenly crumbled at my feet. I prayed and hoped they were all right. There was not a wince from my little princess Valerie Ann, she didn't stir and I was suddenly overcome by a rush of panic feeling drained with fear and anxiety. I reached for them both and to my utter relief Valerie had not absorbed the slightest injury. She peered up at me from her wrapped Welsh fitting and at that moment I remember seeing stars as I am sure Dorothy did too, but for different reasons. Fortunately, Dorothy got away with only a bruise on her forehead, of which we have a photograph. If that wasn't a miracle, I don't know what was. To think I was going to Africa the next morning.

I left the following morning to meet with the group of fourteen men assigned to me at a ship called *Aointa*. It was an unusual situation, as it was normally an officer with a travel warrant that would be commissioned to undertake the task of accompanying soldiers abroad. My group were a mixture of Welsh, Scottish, Irish and English.

The ship we travelled on was one that had been converted from a pleasure ship. There were approximately 3,000 people aboard from various divisions. There were folk from the army, air force, Red Cross, ambulance and even diplomats, an obvious assortment of divisions.

My charge was to keep the fourteen men assigned to me under control. These sort of trips usually gave rise to some form of rowdiness, with men wanting to drink and get drunk. The reason for this behaviour was that they all knew they were going away for a long time and far from home, but what they didn't know was if they would return in one piece or if at all. Therefore, alcohol and stupor was regarded as a form of escapism and relief if only for a moment before the action that lay in wait for them. I was lucky, I had good lads under my control and didn't have to say more than "Stop now lads!" and they would listen. There was real camaraderie in a situation like that.

We eventually landed in Tunis. Such was the confidence of the command, as not only did it tell me the route to go, it also told where we would finish up, assuming we won the war.

We were to port at the 114 Maintenance Unit, RAF Naples. The Secret Service must have been at work. This was approximately before the end of the war. When we got to Tunis, I knew that my brother-in-law, Ernie, another Parker, but not a relation of mine had been posted there. Ernie was my sister Florence's husband. He was a cockney and he played the piano beautifully. He was a very likeable man and everyone loved him.

Ernie had landed in Tunis six months before me. He had got friendly with some little children the day he got off the boat. Apparently, he lifted a child up, gave him a cuddle and three or four days after that he was taken very ill and died of dip (typhus). It was an extremely infectious disease and there was no way to get him home. Sadly he died within a week of getting there, leaving two children David and Maureen.

To my horror, I was posted to the same place as my brother-in-law in Tunis. When we arrived, we couldn't believe what we saw and heard. People were screaming and shouting, running about panic stricken. There were endless cries of agony and unspeakable scenes of horror.

We arrived to witness a large Red Cross liner which had been deliberately set ablaze by a German bomb. I will never forget the cries and screams of all the poor people on that ship, loaded with wounded soldiers, airmen, diplomats and correspondents. There had been all sorts of people on that ship, not to mention the nurses and doctors who were on duty who tended the sick and wounded. They must have all died as the ship was so far ablaze, it had seemed impossible that such advanced devastation would see fit to spare any lives. I can only describe it as sheer tragedy. It was a dreadful experience for us to have witnessed this tragic loss of life.

My group and I linked up with squadrons going from Tunis to Algiers through desert and sand. We were sometimes in front of the eighth army and at times behind them, all under the command of General Montgomery. The heat was incredible. We would think nothing of being wet through sweat, for beads of sweat rolled down our faces from exposure to the intense heat and as if that was not enough, we were plagued with flies, mosquitoes and insects. It was simply unbearable.

When we got to Algiers, I caught malaria, but fortunately it was a mild form of malaria and the prescribed quinine tablets restored me to former health. I do, however, remember the symptoms of drifting into a state of delirium when I had first got the malaria.

The Squadron that we were attached to went on to Tripoli, although I am not certain. We travelled from one country to another, with only road blocks as our blind guide. I say blind guide, as there were no road signs and we just had to hope at each barrier we approached that they were British or American. We followed the Squadrons right through to Monte Cassino where we encountered a terrible battle.

We kept taking it, losing it and taking it again. My goodness, the Germans put up a fight there.

From Monte Cassino we went across to Sicily, raided Sicily and then went on to Italy, where we had quite a fight. It was toward the end of the war. It must have been around the middle of 1945, perhaps a little earlier. When we arrived in Italy, I got to the MU unit in Naples with my crew. It was fortunate that all the men under my command returned home safely. The fourteen I took out with me all came home with me.

Italy had been a challenge, as it was difficult to identify the enemy, because the Italians and the Germans would often dress up in each other's uniforms, so this completely confused us. Fortunately, I managed to get through without any scratches or bullet marks.

When I was in Naples, I was very near a village called Monopoli, the Italians called it Monop. This was about six months before I was due to go home and I thought of all the danger I had been in, what with the boat and the desert.

I wasn't sure when my luck would run out on me and the thought that I was going to get killed was not far from mind, as so many people around me had met their fate. I thought about how lonely I felt and of my need to make friends with somebody for my own protection and sanity. I missed my family and had been away at war for so long.

I did meet a wonderful Italian family that I became friendly with. The mother was Maria. She was quite old and had been through hell with the Germans. Her husband had been killed by the Germans and she was on her own bringing up five girls. They were a tremendous family and welcomed me making me feel very much at home. I enjoyed many a hearty meal of pasta accompanied by the traditional glass of vino with our meal.

I got quite acquainted with the eldest daughter Franca and we enjoyed the simplicity of each other's company. Franca's younger sister, a little madam decided that she would write to my wife and tell her I was having an affair with her older sister. My wife and I corresponded with a letter each way, but she never questioned or mentioned my acquaintance with Franca. I guess she knew, as I did, that she could have got a telegram at any time saying I had been killed. It was very dangerous in Italy, and for your own safety, it was better if you knew someone Italian, as they would keep their eyes open for you and take great care of you. They loved the RAF.

I continued to correspond with my wife and she knew that she was my one and only. My adopted Italian family continued to look out for me. These were such wonderful people; they went as far as tailoring a suit in lovely Italian cloth for me. I was measured up and although I protested, a light grey suit was soon stitched up for me to wear. It was a fine and elegant suit that fitted me like a glove. What craftsmanship these folk possessed. I felt grand in this suit, but I knew

I couldn't really wear it because we had to wear our uniforms and I was afraid to disobey orders.

My protest to wear the suit publicly other than my uniform fell on deaf ears as my Italian family assured me that by the time they finished dressing me up, I would be easily regarded a true Italian. For the first time I allowed myself to be influenced, as deep within, I really wanted to wear this fine suit. So here I was being fussed over by my adopted Italian family, kitting me out with a fine suit, straw boater, sunglasses and a silk scarf to wrap around my neck. True to their word, I looked the part and I bravely strutted as did all other Italians up and down the parade, hours on end on Sunday afternoons. To say the least, the experience was quite exhilarating. Jim Parker the Italian Englishman! My Italian family, they sure did look out for me.

The end of the war was announced. I was demobbed and returned home from the war. At the time I was in the Air Force NAAFI. We felt victorious as we all returned in one piece and as a whole unit. Several of my troops put me up on their shoulders and carried me for about 100 yards. They sang all the way down. They were saying "Corporal Parker, born leader and survivor". The men thanked me and I said a small prayer to thank Jesus for looking out for us all.

I arrived at Kings Cross station with two kitbags. One was full of my uniforms and other equipment and the other contained my ceremonial uniform and all my goodies. There was a gold ring that Dorothy had given me; I think there was a watch; I also know there were wedding photographs I had taken from home and intended to bring back; I had other photographs and gifts for Dorothy and Valerie. We had to put the kitbags onto a station luggage trolley where they collected all the luggage from the train. The trolley was loaded down with kitbags. When we were told to collect them, my second kitbag was gone. We never did find out what had happened to it, never!

I was awarded the Africa Star, the Atlantic Star and the Italy Star for my service in each of these arenas, as well as a Service Medal and a Victory Medal (Left to right in the next plate).

War was over and I was granted the end of war six week leave. The RAF had been my occupation since 1939 and in six weeks time after my leave was over, what was I to do? I sat down to discuss this with Dorothy. After a few weeks Dorothy suggested I approach Eddie next door. Eddie was Dorothy's brother-in-law, a builder who worked on a government project building temporary makeshift houses. Eddie was happy to oblige and he managed to get me in on the project.

Jim's medals

l to r:

The Africa Star, the Atlantic Star and the Italy Star for service in each of these arenas, and the Service Medal and Victory Medal.

LEARNING RESOURCES CENTRE
WARDEN PARK SCHOOL,
BROAD STREET, CUCKFIELD,
HAYWARDS HEATH, SUSSEX
RH17 5DP

3

POST WAR LIFE

The housing project we worked on was designed to meet the demand for accommodation for the many returning from war. It was a simple build-for-speed setup made of concrete panels. Each panel had four grooved sides that would slot one into the other. These houses weren't ideal, but they were a solution in a time of need. We worked like clockwork erecting these grooved panels that weren't always flush or by any means airtight. We'd have to go around pointing the gaps with a very thin trowel and cement to stop draughts seeping through. We found it easier to use our finger to finish off the cement, it looked much neater. I only had a few weeks on that project and had to think of an alternative as the project soon came to an end. I told Dorothy that I intended to go back to the Air Force, as a job there could qualify us for married quarters.

Dorothy was always supportive and encouraging and so I wrote to the RAF seeking employment. I received a letter back from them saying that they didn't need anybody anymore in peacetime.

I was faced with a dilemma of what to do now that I was home from the RAF. There was no time to sit and ponder as I was not one to sit about anyway. After all, I had my wonderful wife Dorothy who believed in me and I wanted to keep her happy and proud of me. I decided I would write to apply for a correspondence course in cost accounting. The advantage of doing the course meant that I would be awarded a diploma and hopefully that would help me get a decent job. The course was new and had been recently launched and encouraged by the government.

After the Second World War, the Government knew that the rebuild of London and its many cities was going to be a costly exercise. They needed a carefully thought-through strategy so as to have total control over spend. It was important to rebuild the cities, encourage manufacturing and to kick-start the exportation of goods from Britain. That was one of the many ways we could get money back as a country since we owed so much to the Americans. Evidently, the World Trust Fund was in a state.

Training folk in various professions, cost accountants being one of the newer courses was essential and important to the Government. Educating the nation after years of war was part of their strategy to rebuild and put the country back on its feet.

I applied for the course and when doing so I found out that you could either qualify as a professional or as an amateur. I applied for the amateur course as I could not afford the professional course. It was very expensive.

Years later though I met with someone who did the professional course and he informed me that there was no difference between the professional or amateur course except that of the price.

I started my course and my wife Dorothy would help me because I didn't know anything at all about maths. Dorothy taught me up to the stage of algebra after which stage I had to self-teach. She was wonderful and patient and I quickly grasped the key principles of maths and studied each night till the early hours of the morning to truly understand my course. It was quite an intense course, but I soldiered on. Cost accounting had an angle different to that of a finance accountant. The difference being that finance accountants would cost goods after they were made, resulting in a loss and cost accountants had to cost a product from inception to end. Time, production and material, and every part of the products had to be calculated to arrive at a total cost.

I got to good grips with my course and got my first job which was working for a carpet manufacture called William Goodacre. They were based in the East End of London right next to the Albert Dock.

My first boss was a very large hearty man. If I remember correctly, I believe he was Jewish. He was the Company Secretary. We discussed the company and its projections and he told me that he had been trying to work out a selling price for the carpets per square yard which he had achieved, but really wanted a truer value based on other factors. Of course he was delighted when I told him I was training to become a cost accountant. In that decisive moment, I was hired and he immediately set to work. I was given all the relevant data pertaining to carpet manufacture to prepare a cost data sheet for us to work from. There were various considerations before reaching a realistic cost of each carpet. One had to consider the type of yarn, its weight and quality. Then there were the sizes, the patterns, the weight of carpets, the length and width, the depth. Sometimes it got complicated, because you then had to calculate production time, machine reliability, as well as the cost in event of time lost in production due to breakdowns or any inconsistencies. I had to calculate the 'IF' factor, variables and non variables. It seemed complicated at first, but the end result was rewarding to be in a position to achieve and deliver such in-depth reporting. The facts and figures of Wilton and Axminster carpets buzzed in my head. I had become so acquainted with my skill and profession that I developed the ability to run figures off the top of my head without having to consult my data sheets if I was questioned off-the-cuff about any form of costing.

I say rewarding since I started my life not knowing how to read or write properly, let alone understand maths. My poor health as a boy kept me from attending school. Then, the war started and I was immediately commissioned abroad, so no real time to study till the war ended. I did feel proud of myself for having achieved such an aptitude for figures and I thank my wife for helping me get there.

William Goodacre's was a family business. I regarded Mr Goodacre as a typical Company Secretary with a good head for business and good values. We got on and he treated me well. He was an understanding man and respected the work I did. As I progressed within my role as cost accountant, the responsibilities increased as did the respect. In fact Mr Goodacre and I became quite friendly. We had a good working relationship.

I remember one Friday afternoon, about 4.30 pm he said to me, Jim! I've had a rough week I think I'll go home early – it's Friday night."

I said, "Yes sir!"

"Now look," he said, "you might as well pack up your desk and come off too. We both deserve a rest." So he went, I packed up my desk, locked up and went to London Bridge. When I got to London Bridge I bought a paper, as normal, to catch my train home which was then New Addington, just outside of Croydon. Croydon council had given us a house in Addington after we'd got married, and Dorothy and I lived on the third floor in Campbell Road.

Anyway, I left the office and seated myself on my train bound for Croydon. As I sat there reading my paper, I lowered my paper to observe the people around me and for no apparent reason, I peered across to gaze into the train stationed alongside my train headed in the same direction. I curiously observed the people in that train too. Some sat there stony faced and without expression, some simply wore a face of anticipation for the train to get a move on and some simply gazed into thin air. The gentleman that sat shoulder to shoulder immediately opposite my window read his newspaper. I guess I was staring into the other train carriage for some time, simply observing the folk and probably wondering after some of the expressive faces. The man reading the paper started to lower his paper and in doing so he looked across into the carriage where I sat. Well, I'll be damned; who do you think it was, it was my boss! What a coincidence. We had worked and became friends, but it never occurred to us that we went home via the same station each day or what train each caught. The next Monday morning we had a good chuckle. What a small world we live in!

It had taken me four years to complete and qualify as a cost accountant. There had been forty people on this correspondence course and only thirty-seven of us passed. When I got this diploma, it qualified me in six subjects, cost accounting, financial accounting, auditor, book-keeping and in commercial mathematics. This diploma was stamped by the BI, the British Institute then, as opposed to the BTI now. That stamp was a leaded stamp which you get on all official documents which was the seal of the British Institute. That was quite a valuable document, although I was not considered a professional as I had sat the cheaper version of the course.

With my qualification firmly under my belt and with a good four years of experience in accountancy, I decided to move on from Goodacre's. I applied for a position at a company called Powers Samas. I think they belonged to the group of I.C.T. International Computers and Tabulators.

I.C.T. was the first company to produce punchcard accounting. A punchcard was like a clock card, all ruled, with numbers, depending on what they were required for. Some were ruled with sixty-five columns, if it was a small payroll, it would be forty-five columns. These cards had to be punched in by what they call key operators. Now these girls had timesheets from the men, which showed all their stoppages – if they were late, it was recorded, if they had bonuses, it was there, everything. Absolutely reams of information. The punch operators had to put this into the cards in the relevant places. After that they would get punched again by what they called the verifiers. They had to be punched twice to make sure they were correct. From there they went to a sorter, which was like a post office sorter that sorted through them all very quickly, into any order. Then they went from there to a tabulator, where they were produced in continuous paper like that of computer printout paper and they usually finished up about a quarter of an inch thick, which when unfolded was quite long. After that procedure they had to be priced up to the office and translated into cash.

I worked for Powers Samas approximately four years. During my travels from London Bridge to Canning Town near Albert Dock, I came to recognise the usual faces and people who board the same train and carriage each day. I became friendly with one particular passenger with whom I'd exchange interesting commentary on various issues and events.

In one of our many conversations, we had discussed our jobs and location. He was a professional cost accountant. How interesting I thought, meeting up with someone in the same profession as mine. Anyway, he was a friendly man and so was I. Bob and I soon become train buddies and would also walk across London Bridge every morning together.

It was quicker to walk across the bridge, than to wait for a bus to get to the other side, as they were always so busy. It seemed a long walk over the bridge to and from work each day, but it was good exercise.

Bob and I got on like a house on fire and having become quite friendly, he invited me to go wrestling with him at Croydon Wrestling Hall. He told me he attended once a fortnight and that it was a simple gathering of chaps messing and throwing each other about. It's nothing serious he had explained and no one gets hurt. I did go with Bob and true to his word, it was as comical and enjoyable as he had told me.

The contenders would come out banging their chests, some very fat men, some well built and even some very good-looking men. I really enjoyed the event and Bob and I would go there religiously every fortnight. It really took you into another world. Being there was a good form of therapy after a hard day's work crunching numbers. It was our moment of escapism and relaxation from the usual everyday occurrences.

By now, we had been friendly for quite some time and Bob asked me to work for him as his assistant accountant. The job he offered was not based in the City with him. He needed someone to work for their sister company called APV, Aluminium Plant and Vessel Company. They were based in Deptford, and I had to transfer it all into a new factory in Croydon.

Bob was keen to have me on board and explained the requirements and perks that went with the job. I remember him apologising for the circumstances of the job in hand and that I'd be given a blank canvas. In short, there would be no desks or staff, just an empty space in Deptford. I would have to use of a makeshift table till the furniture or equipment arrived.

The perks included a good salary and a five bedroomed house. The job was to plan and design the Crawley offices and machinery room in a given space. The task was to ensure a design that would accommodate all the equipment and staff. I also had to calculate overall costs of every department for offices located between Deptford and Crawley.

I accepted the conditions, after all it was a temporary situation and an interesting challenge for me to undertake. The APV job kicked off with me sitting on my makeshift table drawing and drafting my plan. I made models of desks, cabinets, machinery and equipment to plan the move, so that when everything arrived, it would all fit like a glove.

My family and I moved to Crawley into our five bedroomed house! It was at 42 Lady Margaret Road, Ifield. Conveniently located on the corner of Lady Margaret Road was an elementary school called Sarah Robinson. This is where I enrolled my children to be educated; it couldn't have been more comfortable.

I completed the design for the Aluminium Plant and Vessel Company. We only had one machine room operating punch cards for computing wages. We made vessels for the Milk Marketing Board and the brewery industry. The foundry had to be costed and added to the prices of the parts they were making. There was a different foundry casting for every different piece of equipment required to make the infused vessels out of stainless steel or aluminium which held thousands of gallons of beer or milk.

When the vats were completed, they'd be transported to destinations on long trailers. It was a neat operation and costing them from the start to finish was an integral part of the process. The product would arrive from Sheffield in stainless steel form and leave our premises as a finished product. My staff and I did a time and motion study of every item that was made. I stayed with APV for four years and then decided to move on.

I joined Stone Chance. Stone Chance was a company that had been amalgamated from J Stone to Chance Brothers. J Stone manufactured small and big transformers and Chance Brothers made all the optics for lighthouses and beacons. They were international suppliers of their product worldwide.

Consistent with all my other jobs my staff and I would cost account as was the procedure for all manufacturing. I had had quite a large workforce under my supervision at APV and at Stone Chance there were two or three clerks. In fact, I had three of my former staff from APV write to me asking me to employ them.

Angus Langton and Jim Rob eventually left APV to join me at Stone Chance and Ken Stone decided he had more prospects to stay where he was. I had been working unsupervised for Stone Chance for five years, when I was called into the office one day to be informed that the company was restructuring and decided to employ a manager to oversee my team and me. I didn't take lightly to this decision especially since I had successfully run the division for the last five years. In my opinion I didn't need a manager to manage me; I was suitably qualified and did a fine job. I submitted my resignation with no hesitation. I knew I'd find similar work easily enough. I had really felt offended by this new decision and over the period of resignation I took two to three weeks sick leave, something I hadn't done in the five years I worked for Stone Chance.

It was on a fine day during my sick leave when my wife asked me to run up to Crawley town centre on an errand. I jumped into my car and drove off. On my way home, driving through the High Street, I noticed a white Austin Cambridge in front of me. It was actually a taxi, with Barkers of Three Bridges signed on the top of the hood. For some reason or the other, I decided to follow the taxi as I wondered at the prospect of being a taxi driver. When the Austin Cambridge eventually pulled into a cab rank situated at the old level crossing in Crawley, I pulled in behind him. I approached him and enquired about how he became a taxi driver and if there were any vacancies. He pointed me to the office and advised me to chat to old Jack, his boss. He said Jack had been looking for drivers. It was only a five minute interview and since I had a clean licence and no police record I was immediately engaged. I knew Crawley well, so I wasn't worried about getting lost on my trips, beside, as Jack said 90% of the time the passenger directed you anyway.

As a taxi driver, I had some wonderful experiences, like the time I had a call out to go to the Queen Victoria Hospital in East Grinstead. I was instructed to go into the hospital and ask for the surgeon. I thought it strange at the time, because one usually collected passengers outside, but this time I had to go in and ask for a particular surgeon.

I went in, asked for the surgeon who eventually emerged with a square box. It must have been about a nine-inch cubed box, quite heavy and very cold. I was instructed to deliver this box to a hospital up in London. The surgeon handed the box to me and asked me to wait for the police escort to arrive. To say the least, I was intrigued and very curious.

Four policemen arrived and I immediately asked what the purpose of the escort was, when they could have taken the parcel themselves without me piggy-in-the-middle. They explained that they were not insured to carry body parts but had to escort me to deliver the package safely.

It was a nightmare drive from East Grinstead to London zooming past all the traffic lights – red or green, with sirens wailing and lights flashing. I had to turn my lights on full beam and with a police car behind me and one in front of me we departed with a distinct cavalcade. Sirens wailing and lights flashing we travelled at speed not usually permitted to the ordinary driver.

My anxiety and fear didn't subside till I reached our destination. I worried at each crossing that a car would emerge and crash into me soon after the first police car zoomed past a red traffic light. Fortunately that never happened. I don't know how long it took but we seemed to get to London in double quick time, and finally the nightmare drive was over. I delivered the heavy, iced box to the anxious recipients. What an ordeal.

Another experience was a murder case of a young lady whose life was tragically ended when she was killed by someone on her train journey between Crawley and Horsham Station. They found her body in Horsham and a police investigation was launched. Every taxi driver in Crawley was interviewed. Police wanted to know whether any of the drivers remembered picking up a man with certain characteristics.

He was described as dangerous and we were told to observe certain behaviours of our passengers in an effort to identify the suspect. Apparently this character would never sit upfront in the passenger seat alongside the driver which was the norm back in that day and would prefer to sit at the back. We were given a rough description of what he looked like and they told us to be vigilant.

Fortunately I didn't pick anyone matching his description, but I did encounter some very funny passengers, such as the one chap I picked up who didn't know where he lived. He'd had so much drink he kept saying to me, "I think it's here." So I'd pull up, he'd look and say, "No it's not here." He did this about three or four times, realising that I was not going to get any money out of this chap, so I stopped the car, opened the door and told him to get out of my car and find his own way home.

One of the things I did on an early shift was to take my children over to the back of Lowfield Heath to the emergency access gate for ambulances and fire engines at Gatwick Airport. There was no sign prohibiting pedestrians, so I'd take my children to this locked barbed wire gate from which we would plane spot. Each of them would have their little pads and a pencil to take down plane numbers and airline names. It was an exhilarating experience for the children observing these huge planes lift into the air. They contented themselves being able to spot the numbers and names and excitedly scribble down their observations.

It was delightful watching them. Their little faces would light up with glee as they'd compare and exchange notes. Aaah! What vivid warm memories I have of my five angels. They were happy times, with memories of love, togetherness and unity never afar from mind. The 'greats' have to be the memory of their individual little characters and how they'd look out for each other. Even today they still look out for each other despite living huge distances apart.

I took pride after my children's simplicity and how they learnt to appreciate and give value to the little things in life. Content and never demanding, but strong willed to do well and reach goals matched to their strengths. And if by chance one of the siblings lagged behind, there was always a mustering and a ready hand to reach out and help. How I loved spending time with my children and watching them grow from strength to strength.

We loved our plane spotting and I once took them to our favourite spot after a fresh downfall of snow. This was a first for them and they quizzed me about being able to see the runway since it would be covered with snow. "Don't worry," I said and hurried them to put their coats and scarves on. As they dressed up, I explained that there would be a snow plough. We made our way to Gatwick and sure enough they were snowploughing the runway.

It was a fantastic scene of red green and blue lights marking the different gateways for landed planes or ones ready to take off. The snowplough created a huge spray of thin snow and we could see the lovely lights shining through it. We all gazed in wonderment, absorbing the atmosphere. At that moment, I wondered what it would be like being able to work at an airport.

There was something so captivating about an airport; it made you want to be there. I held the thought. Up until then, the closest I got to an airport apart from our regular plane-spotting outings was my regular fare every morning from a chap called Brian. I'd have to drive him each morning from Crawley Station to Gatwick, and then bring him back to Crawley in the evenings. I did this journey everyday for about fourteen months.

4

GATWICK AIRPORT

Brian was an interesting man. He possessed this air of confidence that was neither aloof nor arrogant. I liked Brian as despite his upright and steady temperament he also seemed to be an easy-going sort of chap. Probably an influential man I had thought, but if so, never boastful in character or demeanour. Our conversations had always been simple, often about sport, weather, airplanes and occasionally war. He was never too chatty or enquiring. The most personal question he had presented was when he asked what I'd done previous to taxi driving. He had chuckled at my sudden ninety-degree turn in career but said nothing more. I knew it was just a casual small talk question and thought nothing of it; neither did it occur to me that my previous experience could be of any interest to him in the slightest.

Like clockwork, I picked Brian up each morning and evening to take him back and forth to Gatwick. On one of my trips accompanying Brian to work, he said to me with easy manner, "Jim, you've been a cost accountant, what the hell are you doing driving a taxi? Have you got any idea what these men over at the airport earn?" He continued, "You're earning peanuts, why don't you get a job at the airport?"

"You're joking," I said. "I've never seen a job advertised at the airport."

"I'll give you a job," Brian offered. I chuckled back saying "You're having a laugh. You're joking right!"

"No I'm not. If you want a job at the airport, I can explain the job description now."

"Go on then!" I challenged, feeling pretty elated.

"Well," he went on to explain, "it would begin with you driving a three-ton truck loaded with equipment or hot food." Your job would be to drive them round the gates finding the aircraft, X-ray India or Whisky Tango or whatever and deliver the equipment or the hot food. It would be a totally different job for you and I have no doubt in your ability, you certainly don't seem fazed to do any job and this one will get your foot in the door. You'll get some help and you'll nearly always have a driver with you who will show you the way and the ropes, I think you'll enjoy it."

I was convinced that Brian was joking. "I'm not joking Jim, I'll give you a job tomorrow morning if you want one, but you'll have to fill in an application form and put down everything you've learned. In my opinion you won't have to stay very long doing this job. With your experience, you'll soon be on your way up the ladder, trust me!" I thanked him and dropped him off at Gatwick.

Jim Parker was not one to waste time or look

a gift horse in the mouth. An airport job! They were hard enough to come by let alone have them dropped wham-bam into your lap. Well I'll be damned if I'd mess up on this opportunity. I hurried home to share the great news with my family. My job as a taxi driver ended there and then and the very next day I reported to Brian's office to complete my application and start my new job.

I had two to three weeks training and got to working on the trucks delivering or returning the casings back and forth. The cars would return to base with packets of unused coffee or teabags to which the lads would help themselves and take home. Not wanting to be a goody-goody, I too would help myself to the selection of unused coffee and teabags. It seemed to be the norm and no one appeared to frown or express alarm if one took some coffee or a few tea bags.

Not long into my job as a truckie, a job notice for someone in stores was posted on the staff board in the casing department. Brian called me up and asked if I wanted to move off the trucks. He encouraged me to apply for the position particularly since I had accounting experience. My application was successful and I was put on the night shift. My job was to pack each flight separately; they were all different depending where they went. Some flights went as far as Lagos or Accra, some flights only to Belfast or Glasgow or the Channel Islands. I would be on one side of stores during my night shift, and a young lady would be on the other side of stores packing up kits which were applicable to each of the different aircrafts.

I had got acquainted with my new job very quickly, the operation was easy and although repetitive and potentially boring, I executed my duties efficiently as was the norm for whatever I did.

It was about 3 am one morning when I noticed a gentleman enter the stores. My colleague and I had been busy carrying out our shift and didn't stop to look up. From the corner of our eyes, we both watched this smart looking gentleman casually walk into stores. We thought that this was perhaps a sort of management walk-about routine overseeing that shift staff wasn't loafing.

He looked quite old, small built and a very smart gentleman. He wore a little wax moustache and for the small man he was held himself up pretty tall. My colleague and I exchanged glances but said nothing, as we continued to work. Of course, apart from our assumption about him doing some kind of walkabout, we did wonder quite quizzically who the devil he was. This was not the sort to come down to stores!

He had a good look around before actually walking over to where I was standing. "Excuse me," he politely enquired, "Are you Mr Jim Parker?" He introduced himself as Mr Sheriff.

After our exchange of pleasantries, Mr Sheriff asked in a very direct and confident manner, "Mr Parker, How would you like to be my accountant."

A thought hit my mind, and I smiled inwardly. "*Another gift horse!*" And without hesitation I replied "I'd love that sir!"

He spoke with quite a full on heavy-set plum accent. "I've read your application form and you're just the man I'm looking for." He stroked my ego as he went on to acknowledge the wealth of my experience and qualifications. "You have vast experience and people of your calibre are very rare." I was enjoying the flattery and thought, "go on then, don't stop," and he did continue. "Your choices of work have been varied and diverse, this gives a strong impression of versatility and adaptability. I can't say with certainty that I'd have been as brave to undertake some of the tasks you did, but lets talk this over at my home on Saturday around about 10 to 10.30 a.m. My home is in Chichester, will you come over there? I'm not too bothered about an exact timing, but do come and we can sit and discuss the job. I'll just quickly tell you that there are a few complications, but I'm sure you will understand once I explain them. The job is yours if you want it; just a few issues and requirements I need to clarify and understand if you are agreeable." I arranged to be at his home on the Saturday at about 10.30 a.m.

Mr Sheriff left and I finished my shift and went home to tell my wife. I had thought to myself, it appears that my luck always came with a price. Would I always be faced with the *gift horse* saddled with some form of minor *complication*? That seemed to be the case with most of my jobs. It was always a case of having to give in order to receive.

Saturday came and I went over to see him. When I first got to his door I thought, well this can't be his house as the front door is right on the pavement. I got my piece of notepaper out to check his address and sure as rain, I was at the right address. I rung the bell, and was greeted by a sweet old lady.

"Are you Mr Jim Parker?"

"Yes Madam."

"Come in, my husband is waiting for you."

She showed me in and I was greeted heartily by Mr Sheriff. He turned to his wife and asked her to pour me a whisky. Whisky was hardly what I expected at half past ten in the morning and I wondered how I'd cope since I wasn't really a whisky man. She poured what looked like a double shot to me.

"For goodness *sake* woman!" he exclaimed, *"TIP THE BOTTLE UP!"* She filled my glass right up to the top and handed it to me. The thought of drinking the stuff horrified me. I hate whisky and the only way I could drink it was to hold my nose and pour it down my throat and swallow damn hard.

Of course, I couldn't do that and I was dreading the moment when we'd have to exchange salutations and I'd have to graciously take my first sip. Thoughts of stupor reeled through my mind. This is the part that Jim Parker had to somehow muster up courage to honour the heads up without splattering and convulsing at the smell.

By George, if only Sheriff knew, I'd be drunk and staggering out of his home after two sips let alone a full glass. There was no way in high heaven I was going to drink more than a sip because no doubt he'd refill my glass thinking I was a seasoned drinker by which time, I'd probably need an ambulance. He'd no sooner withdraw his job offer if I staggered out of his home. His impression of me as a versatile and adaptable man was going to stick and I wasn't about to negate my good image with a glass of whisky. I knew that more than one sip would easily hold me ransom, so I carefully nursed my whisky picking it up pretending to raise it to my lips but then a response to a question he presented would conveniently allow me to replace the whisky back on the side table whilst I replied.

We raised our glasses to exchange salutations, and he started to tell me about the job he wanted to offer me.

"I've got a wonderful job for you", he announced in his posh voice. He went on to tell me about how he met Freddie Laker at an exclusive gentleman's club up in London. The two of them had got talking about their careers and past experiences.

Mr Sheriff had been retired for the last five years. He had been a Budget Control Officer for the Queen's Own Light Regiment in the army during World War I, and later promoted to Financial Director in industry.

Mr Sheriff told Freddie Laker that he had been responsible for the financial budgeting of all operations relating to a brigade of about two thousand men. He explained the job as being massive and that everything relating to the war, used or needed, be it housing or medical had to be accounted for, costed and then released for supply.

Mr Sheriff had told Freddie Laker that the government provided a budget for each regiment and that he had to operate within the strict parameters. I listened with great interest as Mr Sheriff sipped at his whisky and talked me through his conversation with Freddie Laker.

It emerged that Mr Sheriff and Freddie Laker shared a common interest in catering. Mr Sheriff owned three restaurants in Mayfair London. Freddie Laker took great delight in this information and propositioned Sheriff to come out of retirement and handle the Gatwick Catering Unit he owned. "I'm enjoying my retirement", Sheriff told me and I think this would be a perfect job for you.

Since Sheriff was not interested in Freddie Laker's proposal to run the catering unit at Gatwick, he had promised and agreed to find a suitable candidate to meet his needs. He went on to explain that Gatwick Catering although fully equipped with staff and kitchen, had to use external caterers, namely The Marriot and Trust House Forte. These caterers provided limited and unsatisfactory service. Freddie Laker wanted to find someone suitably qualified to develop and run an internal catering unit that would meet his company objectives in terms of supply, cost and operation.

The Gatwick Catering Company enjoyed a monopoly of the market as they were the only unit serving all the domestic and international flights. The unit wasn't ideally located and was situated next to BEA and the BOAC. However, despite the major noise problems the staff endured from the engines, it was a fully-fledged operation with potential to increase turnover if only it did it own catering. The operation already employed a staff of seven chefs and a general workforce of about two-hundred people. With the backing of a ready-to-go trained workforce, it made sense to develop an internal catering unit.

Freddie Laker knew that the set up would require someone capable and willing to take on the responsibility. He couldn't do it himself as he ran other businesses. He needed to employ someone to initiate and activate the process. This someone had to be qualified on paper with experience to match in terms of diversity, cost accounting capabilities, adaptability and pure dedication.

I had taken in the entirety of Sheriff's conversation with Freddie Laker. Mr Sheriff looked at me as if to search my face for enthusiasm. He stood up, walked over to the drinks cabinet to refill his glass with whisky. When he returned to the comfort of his leather settee, he leaned back, crossed his legs and continued to regard me with what seemed like an approving grimace. "Mr Parker," he declared, "this is a job for you. I was lucky to have come across your CV."

I was happy to have been so highly regarded, but he still hadn't yet disclosed the underlying issues he had mentioned when we first met at stores.

Mr Sheriff sipped at his whisky then spoke. "The problem I'm faced with though is that your CV is so good, I daren't let the other accountants or the Financial Director know about you." He uncrossed his legs, leaned forward and spoke earnestly but in a whisper to emphasise the severity of what he was about to tell me.

"If the Accountant or the Financial Director find out about your experience, they will want you down in their offices immediately. There is nobody in that unit to match your capability, and I shall lose you. What I've got to do is hide you from everyone in BUA (British United Airways). There is enough money to pay you as a junior manager, but I want you to work as a senior manager. It gets complicated!" he continued. "If I put you as a senior manager, the Financial

Director himself would arrange your salary and he would come to know who you are. If I leave you as a junior accountant, it's only the Chief Accountant that would arrange your salary and he would take no notice. My dilemma is that I simply don't want to lose you Jim. You're a pot of gold to me!" exclaimed Mr Sheriff.

"I'm not going to beg you. You can please yourself Jim. I'll understand if you refuse, but I hope you'll take my offer."

"Don't worry sir, you've told me enough. I will take it. It would be a wonderful experience and a challenge that I look forward to taking on board."

"Done deal then, Mr Parker," and with that we raised and clinked our glasses. Did I sip the whisky on that? Not even a bit. I left soon after.

I reported to a lady called Katie the following Monday morning. She worked for the Operations Director. The Operations Director was the most important director of the whole airline industry, because everyone under his management had contact with the public and keeping the public happy was a very important marketing tool.

I started my job as a junior manager after having reported to Katie. We got on real fine. She used to wait for me every morning for us to have coffee together. Katie wouldn't have coffee without me. I would arrive at work, go straight to the office to leave my briefcase and hang my coat, and then make my way to Katie's office to have coffee with her. This became a routine that lasted from the time I joined in 1966 to 1971.

In 1971 Freddie Laker sold the unit to Caledonian Airways, a Scottish airline. They were one hundred per cent union, a pro-shop union. They came in, took over and made changes. All the hostesses had to have a Scottish uniform. Originally they had the Laker uniform with a nice cream and blue colour. The Caledonian style had obviously changed to kilts and Scottish uniform. Everybody had to be re-equipped with the Caledonian brand.

I have worked for the catering department between the years 1966 to 1971. It had been a huge responsibility and I managed several staff from operations including eight cost clerks reporting to me. There were two on the bought ledger; two on the sales ledger, two floating, then I had a comptometer operator and sometimes a secondary.

My work was done by the chief typist who sat in a typing pool. She was also responsible for most of the director's work and mine. I did all this under cover – nobody knew that I was in fact a senior manager. I attended the meetings with the senior managers, Norman and Bob. Bob was in charge of all the traffic that meant everything other than the hostesses. There'd be all kinds of hostesses, four hundred ground staff reporting to Norman (a senior manager) and four hundred air staff reporting to the Operations Director, they were all chosen because of their capability to represent the airline, both in elegance, appearance and particularly for the way they dealt with passengers.

One of the perks working for B.U.A. was the opportunity of a free flight for you and your family to any destination. The only drawback was that they were never guaranteed. If you took advantage of the free travel, submitted your application form and it was approved, the underlying rule was that paying passengers had priority over your travel arrangements and that they could be cancelled or interrupted at any stage of your trip in the event of seat shortage.

Our first trip was to Australia for all seven of us. We just got lucky, because it was next to impossible to have seven empty seats that B.U.A. workers could take advantage of. We enjoyed a lovely holiday in Australia and the children were all very good. On the way back to London we hit the jackpot again and all seven of us were allowed to board the plane. However, when we got to Kuala Lumpur we were politely asked to get off. We were put into a lovely hotel, so it was really like a stopover holiday for the children. It was scorching hot and the kids enjoyed the swimming pool. It was an absolutely fantastic hotel, quaint and full of eastern promise.

My wife and I were enjoying a walk in the gardens of the beautiful hotel we'd been put up in, when we heard someone say, "Eh! Weren't you on the flight yesterday? What happened to you then?" I explained to him that we were pulled off the flight without our luggage. "Good Lord, how unfortunate," he retorted. "We'll have to have a whip a round and see how much we can raise between us to get you some change of clothing and a few other bits and pieces." He pointed towards his colleagues. They were a group of aircrew, the pilot, captain, chief steward and about eight hostesses all in their bathing suits relaxing at the poolside.

It's so rare to find people who possess the 'gift of giving' yet they're out there and over the years my family and I have met many wonderful people. We get so wrapped up in our own worlds and fail to see how we can help others by a simple gesture. Be it a smile, words of encouragement or just a shoulder to lean on. It really doesn't take much and doesn't have to cost anything either.

The group of aircrew kindly whipped up a kitty and gave us some money. They were very helpful indeed.

Three days later, our luck was in and we were lucky to board a flight back home. I wasn't going to let any of my family fly without me. It was either we all got on or all stayed back. The flight desk had already closed, so our hopes sort of ended as we saw the desk attendants pack up.

Suddenly, just before the flight was due to leave, some guy come rushing toward us hurrying us up to walk toward him. He was a local attendant from Kuala Lumpur. "Come on, come one, come on, hurry", he shouted. We rushed toward him and he ushered us onto the flight bound for London. There were seats on the aircraft, but we weren't registered to fly, they knew we had been trying to board and they took a chance and let us on, therefore if there had been a plane crash we wouldn't have been named or listed as being on that flight.

We didn't get to sit together, but the gentleman I sat next to kindly offered to swap seats with my wife so she could be seated beside me. That was another kind gesture I really appreciated.

The children were as good as gold after all we'd been through. We were exhausted when we finally got home, but I never will forget that flight of freedom.

In 1971 I took on extra work, I was made controller of the whole operations division. There were just under five thousand people involved. I was responsible for the whole of the budget in the operations division which included everybody connected to the terminal building. I used to have to go to the terminal building occasionally just to watch, and mingle with the passengers. I dressed smartly, so no one knew who I was. I would walk about as if I was a passenger and observe everything that went on. I'd watch how the baggage control worked, whether they had enough men, whether the check-in girls at the desks were too busy or not, if there were enough of them and if they all worked well together. I did the same with all the loaders, the baggage handlers, the catering people, everybody.

There wasn't a penny spent in that whole department that I wasn't in control of. On my pre-budget forecast I'd send out a letter asking all managers what they anticipated in terms of their requirements for the up coming year. If they did not tell me of an item they needed, then they simply wouldn't get it, they had to be very careful on their budget forecast because my job was to make a profit.

I remember my first board meeting, six months into my job. The board meeting was called to negotiate a new raise rate for the summer season. Once the rate was agreed in a percentage, we'd meet in the operations division. I went to this meeting of about thirty junior, general and senior managers, approximately thirty trade union reps, all the senior ones and myself. They had all been against me but I had to keep the prices and costs down for us to win the award. So we all negotiated, discussing our options and what it would cost if we put on two per cent a year, spread it across thirty people here and forty people there and fifty people somewhere else. All reached for their calculators, sharpened pencils, pens and paper.

It was an atmosphere of determination, seemingly a race against time. I looked across the table to the Operations Director, who sat directly opposite me. "Excuse me, Sir," I called out. He acknowledged me with raised brows and sudden interest. I said to him," Sir, the answer to the calculation is … so and so and so and so."

"Is that Jim Parker?" he said in an authoritative but enquiring manner. "How the devil have you done that? I can't see a calculator there, have you got a magic wand?"

"No, Sir."

"What are you telling me then? Do you have a pencil and paper then?"

"No, Sir."

"Are you telling me that you've done that in your head?" He enquired.

"Yes, Sir, I have."

"Well then, I'm gonna check it." He checked it using his calculator. At this stage, all eyes were focussed on the Operations Director as he calculated away. After a short time, still looking at his calculator, a smile slowly formed across his face and his creased brow loosened, he raised his gaze to address the anxious table of 50 or so glaring eyes and nodded reassuringly to me, he sat up and exclaimed, "This man has not only a clever brain, I will call him a genius. I've never ever had anybody do this in my life." And from then on I did not use any calculator, any pencil and paper, anything at all. I calculated everything in my head.

Sometimes I would attend meetings with Freddie Laker, the Managing Director and

Operations Director. We would discuss strategies of how to enhance our services and capacity. We'd have discussions of how to implement and the effects of customer services versus cost. We discussed the pros and cons of a stretched aircraft and had to calculate facts and figures, and costings of various services, which one to keep and which ones to eliminate. I never ever used a calculator; I calculated everything in my head.

Marketing staff in the catering office would do pages full of figures involving pay the bill ledger which were in units of tens and hundreds. I would go down the page efficiently adding in my head and not be wrong. That was when I was in my prime, but even now I could still do something like that. I had a thoroughly good time doing my job.

I had joined in 1966. In 1968 I asked my son Christopher if he was interested in a job at the airport. "Yes Dad, I'd love that." When I went to work the following day, I asked Katie if I could get Chris a job in one of our many divisions.

I told her how hard he worked as a youngster, how he was doing two paper rounds and helping the butcher on Saturday. I knew he was going to get on, he had all the drive. Katie was always kind and wanted to help. "I can't make that decision Jim; it's too high for me. I'll ask the Operations Director."

Katie phoned the Operations Director whilst I stood in the office; she held the phone to me so I could hear the conversation. She said to the

Director, "Jim Parker wants to know if he can get his son a job in here."

"Yes he can have a job in here. I don't know his son, if Jim wants his son to have a job here, he shall have a job here. If there's any trouble down there with any of the staff I'll be down and bloody well sort them out." And he did do that when there was trouble.

Chris came to work at the airport and over a five-year period he was fully trained and became exceptionally skilled in all areas within the whole catering experience. His skill was tailored and his vision sharp – Chris was a bright young man and I was proud of my son. One of the fundamental tasks he assumed was to write up a manual that covered every aspect from general to what to do in an event of an emergency. This task required vast and sound knowledge of the catering business. He was made a duty officer with all the gold on his hat and his cuffs. There had been four duty officers, he was just another one.

A lot of trouble had brewed over Chris's promotion to duty officer. There had been folk who had been waiting years to get that job, but Chris was appointed. Chris had always excelled in everything he did and was always on the lookout to progress. One day he approached me about a job he saw posted on the sales board for a sales rep. Chris wanted to apply and asked me if he could give it a go. "Well I'll have to ask the Operations Director," I told him.

I called up and discussed Christopher's wish to apply for the sales rep position. The Operations Director was silent for a while, and then he responded with a degree of measure. Somehow, I felt I was being put on the spot and my judgement being discreetly questioned. Was I over stepping my boundaries? I didn't think so; I was doing what I could to help my son progress.

"Jim, if Chris wants a job in sales and you think he can do it, he can be posted there, but I'm trusting that you will make the right decision." Chris transferred to sales on the back of my decision.

I had dedicated twelve years of my life to building this organisation brick by brick, carefully calculating every single move to reach objectives that went far and beyond expectation. Over the years, my fountain of knowledge spilt over with bounty so that all could benefit. I had always been invited to every meeting both general and top management. I don't say I made all the decisions, remember; I had to remain somewhat incognito. It was only at private review meetings that I would be asked to reassess and fine tune the decisions that had been made in the board room.

My saddled gift horse was coming to pass. Twelve years of more responsibility for less than the going rate. Sheriff's words were buzzing in my head, "You're so good, and I can't afford to lose you. I have to hide you from top management. There's enough money to pay you as a junior manager but I need you to work as a senior. You need to play it safe. You're just the man for this job."

It was a Monday morning, not long after my Chris had transferred to his new job. I walked into my office and as I always did, to set down my coat and briefcase, and then make my way to Katie's office.

This Monday was a different Monday. As I walked into my office, there was a young man sitting at my desk, going through my papers!!! Without hesitation and with I imagine a good measure of indignity, words of anger tumbled out! "WHO THE HELL ARE YOU and WHAT THE HELL ARE YOU DOING GOING THROUGH MY PAPERS?"

The boy's body language was arrogant and nonchalant. He did not even stop to address me as he fumbled through my papers. He had even gone as far as having one of my locked drawers opened and had been going through my private paperwork.

He remained oblivious to my distress and regarded me with audacity as he continued to shuffle my papers from left to right. He twisted his mouth and tilted his head and replied in this infuriating drooling and sarcastic manner, seemingly enjoying every bit of my reaction.

"Ah, I've been sent down by the Financial Director to take oooover your job – you need to teach me everything you know, EVERYTHING!!"

"You what?!" I replied

"Yeah! I bin sent down by the financial director to take over your job – you gotta teach me!"

The boy couldn't even speak properly – what the hell was this?

I was enraged and stormed out to Katie's office. "What do you know about this, I'm being replaced?" I hollered. Poor Katie, her expression was regretful and it was evident she knew little.

"Jim, the Operations Director was called into the board meeting on Friday and told that a new employee would assume your position and you would have to work under him. They said if you don't like it, then you can go."

I was flabbergasted and at that moment I felt the strength leave my body. My rage had subsided, but I could still feel the anxiety in my throat. It stung. By now my heart had sunk into the depths of my belly. I could hear the murmur of Katie's voice in the background, but I wasn't making sense of what she was actually saying, it was just background noise as my own head swirled with memories of twelve years of pure dedication. I was being scrapped and tossed aside. I was fifty-eight years old … but, my thoughts were interrupted by Katie shaking me.

"Jim", she said, "Don't resign; whatever you do, don't resign, because if you resign at fifty-eight years of age, the job centre will go crackers. Fifty-eight years old, a cost accountant, you will never get another job. Make them sack you Jim."

She said," All you've got to do is refuse to teach him and they'll sack you."

I had decided and walked back to my office. The boy was still sitting at my desk unperturbed and arrogant as ever. "You've had it mate, I'm not teaching you a damn thing."

"Oh", he said, "I'll tell the Financial Director that you're refusing to help me." He sounded like such a wimp. "YES, young man, I'm not teaching you a damn thing."

I was called up by the Financial Director. He didn't address me; he attacked me with words of disdain and condemnation. "You've been a waste of space for five years Jim Parker, you and your son. We're a company, not a crèche. Your son has been hopping from place to place, never satisfied. When he'd learnt everything that was valuable in the catering department, you then allowed him to go into sales. How long is this going to continue for? Next he'll want my job. What kind of nonsense is that? You have cost the company a lot of money for nothing. As of this moment your employment is terminated, you can pack your bags and leave right now."

I remained calm as I tried to make sense of what he had just lashed out. "Thank you, sir," I replied in a dignified manner and discreetly left the building. My career had ended. No considerations to the profits I delivered or the awards we won over the past twelve years due to careful budgeting and good customer care. I was told that I was a 'waste of space.' I cost the company its profits by allowing my son to progress. That didn't add up. Either way, they fired me because they insisted that my son and I cost them their profits. It was hard to feel anything but anger and when I got home, I took my diploma and ripped it to shreds. I knew I'd never be employed in my profession again, not at fifty-eight years old.

I didn't tell my family that I was fired. I didn't want my son to know it was because of him, so I went home to tell my wife that I'd resigned. I remember the day he called to meet up with him near the catering unit. He begged me to take my job back. He was so innocent. If only he knew that his progress ended my career and there was no way for me to return.

Christopher went from strength to strength in his job in Sales. It had been a wonderful move for him. He mastered everything from sales, swaps, changes, to cancellations. Doing his job with such passion and commitment, Chris was quick on the uptake to recognise a niche in the market when it came to cancellations that resulted in empty seats. He was privy to a lot of information and started to work closely with the sales reps he knew all over the world working for different airlines. He was particularly interested in Viking International where two friends of his worked. On hindsight I guess the financial director who sacked me recognised Christopher's determination and had every reason to shudder.

Christopher eventually left British Caledonian Airways and joined a company called Court Lines based in Luton. He wasn't long in his job when he heard through the grapevine that Court Lines were broke. Chris being Chris seized the opportunity. He contacted his two friends at Viking International and offered to transfer the business of the failing Court Lines to them. His friends at Viking (both named John) offered Chris a position with Viking International and gave him shares. Chris eventually became very successful and bought the two Johns out. They both moved to Jersey and Chris continued to improve his business.

He repackaged Viking to create Unijet moving his operations to Rocky Lane going towards Haywards Heath. On the left was a cottage which was partly owned by the electricity board. Chris had bought the land and he opened an office there which was very, very modern. Everybody enjoyed working there. A supreme office, I've been down there several times, it had every convenience.

I often meet people who have worked for Chris and I listened to all sorts of opinions. Not all were positive, but in life it's not possible to please everyone.

Chris built his company up and eventually in 1998 he sold up for a huge amount of money and became a multimillionaire. The sale of Unijet was widely televised across all the regions. He was awarded entrepreneur of the year 1995.

How can I be anything but very proud of my son? I knew he would push and push and push, until he got what he wanted and he proved me right and there's never anybody in the world happier, more exited to know just how well their son did despite the challenges.

Chris has been very, very good to all the family, none of them have ever had to go out to work Some of them do charity work, some don't, some are abroad but I'm going into all those in detail in the next part of my book. That is really the end of my working life.

5

MY FAMILY

I want to touch on the lives of each individual of my immediate family because every one of them had got a story to tell that is unique.

My father left home when he was in his early twenties. His father was very strict, he was very religious and I think he drove my father away through his strictness, but he didn't move only because his father was strict, he moved also because there was no work for him in Southampton.

My father walked from Southampton to London, I think he linked up with the Jarrow Marchers who were marching to London to beg for work. When he eventually reached London, he met my mother. They courted and not long after, they married. My father never spoke about his childhood or his family members, so I have no relations with any of his Parker family. I don't even know if he had any brothers and sisters. It just wasn't a subject ever discussed in our family. Dad was a very, very proud man.

He spent a lot of time with my children and I'll always remember how the children used to play with him down on the beach at Bognor Regis. They would make a model of a racing car and he would sit in and pretend to drive. Then they would bury him in the sand. He was so easy-going with the children, they adored him. He'd play with them for hours on end.

Those were the good old days, there's nothing like bringing up a family of children. I firmly believe that if you can't enjoy that part of your life, then you don't know how to live. There is nothing more joyful than to see your children grow up. The biggest pain for me was letting go. You just have to hope they're always safe. For those out there with children, I tell you with all my heart, revel, and embrace your children. Love them as they deserve, teach them respect and dignity and be there for them, for when they fly the nest, they will take with them the values you instilled of love and respect for life.

My Father fought in the First World War in the Royal Engineers. He was just an ordinary soldier, no rank but he did receive three medals (left to right in the following plate): a campaign medal for the Battle of The Somme, a World War I Service Medal and a Victory Medal.

I remember when we lived in Wimbledon, we used to go regularly to go see the Armistice Day march from Wimbledon Common down into the Wimbledon High Street. My father was a member of the British Legion and we would watch him marching. He'd be all dressed up in his suit decorated with his three medals. He wasn't a tall man, in fact, he was quite chubby, but when he walked down that hill, he walked proud. My sister and I would wave and cheer as our father marched by. What wonderful memories of pride and joy.

He was so good to me all his life, he had a hard life, and I remember going back to the days when we were in the soup kitchens, dad really tried hard to give me a life. That was my father.

My mother was a bit different to my father, she was a very determined lady; she was very, very kind and very caring. Actually, where I was concerned she tried to wrap me up in cotton wool where she could. She was very protective and I never wanted her to worry about me so much. I just wanted to get better and live a normal childhood. I can't say much about my mother except that she was a very loving wonderful mother. She too was a simple lady and would be content with simple things. Back in those days there were more poor people than there were rich, so folk seemed to fall into that category of simplicity.

She was a dear mum. The only time we ever fell out was when I joined the air force. She was so hurt about that. We resolved our differences and we never fell out like that again.

****

I think my sister Iolanthe Evelyn Parker was named Iolanthe after the comic opera written by Gilbert and Sullivan in the early years. I can't think of any other reason as Iolanthe was not a common name. Speaking on the subject of names, I on the other hand was christened Albert

**Albert Henry Parker. Corporal.
114285.
Royal Engineers.
3rd. Labour Corps. 702 Company.
Served: August 1915 - March 1919.**

Jim's father's medals

l to r:

a campaign medal for the Battle of The Somme,
a World War I Service Medal
and a Victory Medal.

Charles Parker and despite that, I've always been addressed as Jim from the day I was born. If you remember, it was my aunt who came up with the name 'Sunny Jim' because apparently I had been so smiley and Jim has stuck ever since.

Iolanthe was sweet and we got on well as children. As kids we'd play together with my Meccano set. I had gone off to the army at quite an early age, so Iolanthe and I didn't get to spend quality time together. We were in a sense quite close despite our distance. Well, that was up until she changed religion.

I had returned home from the war on my first leave. Iolanthe was jumping about like a little jack rabbit happy to see me. She was excited about something, but wouldn't disclose the full detail.

"Jim, would you like to come up to the Albert Hall with me to see a show."

"Yes, I'd love that, Iolanthe," I replied.

"We don't have the best seats, we're right at the very top, but don't worry, we'll still have fun."

"So what's it about, Iolanthe"? I quizzed her.

"Ah! Don't ask too many questions, just come and you see, you'll love it."

We went to the Albert Hall, and we were almost at the top of the gods. It was quite daunting looking down. The curtains drew back and the band stopped playing. The stage had a table and four chairs. Funny way to start a show, I thought. It didn't take me long to realise that this was no show. This was a Billy Graham Evangelist fiasco signing up people to join his movement.

I remember becoming very angry at her for trying to trick me. No one likes dishonesty or misleading information, least from your immediate family. I couldn't believe my sister tried to lure me in to joining her religion. If she thought she could get me down those stairs to sign up to this religion, she was very wrong. She had misled me into thinking it was a show and I walked out on her leaving her very embarrassed in front of her friends. She ended up signing up to the religion on her own. I had simply refused. I've never forgiven my sister for that stunt, never.

Iolanthe had her good points and she was a brilliant student. She had attended secondary modern school and was awarded a scholarship to attend Wimbledon Grammar school. When she completed her education her first job was as a clerk assistant at Barclays Bank.

She climbed up the corporate ladder and became the first woman in the history of Barclays Bank to become a manager. She was promoted to manager of the Trustees Department that opened in Warminster in Wiltshire. I was very proud of her and felt she was very deserving because Iolanthe was hard-working.

****

My wife Dorothy was born in the Rhondda Valley in the very, very poor part of the coal mining town of Treorchy on the 2nd January

1921. She had seven sisters and four brothers. Dorothy was a very clever girl at school; she was a cut above most schoolgirls at that time. I believe that she was the head girl in her final years at school selected by the headmaster because of her knowledge and presentation. She was also blessed with a wonderful personality and considered an exceptional young lady.

Dorothy's father was a skilled carpenter and joiner. No doubt he had an apprenticeship when he was young. I even remember his lovely old chest of tools out in the carriage at Campbell Road. It was a pirate treasure chest sort of box, very heavy, very thick wood and all around it was a steal wrap. It was just like a pirate's chest. He had all his valuable tools in there and it did have an oilstone where you could sharpen your chisels, which looked like it was donkey's years old because it was given to him by his father. I don't know what has happened to it now.

Dorothy and I got married and had five wonderful children. Valerie arrived first, then Christopher, Michael, Phillip and last was Daryll. A remarkable statistic has been taken from this, as I do wonder how many times the sequence of the days on which they were born would happen. The four boys in age order were born on 17th, 18th, 19th and 20th of the month.

Darryll was born on the 17th, Phillip on the 18th, Michael on the 19th and Christopher on the 20th. That must be unique.

Dorothy, my wife was streets ahead of me in terms of education and she helped me tremendously with everything. I think I met her quite accidentally in the blackout. We were destined to meet and I have never ever stopped loving her regardless of what she thinks. Hand on heart; I will never ever stop loving my Dorothy.

Although I loved Dorothy dearly, one of the things I never did was to call her darling or sweetheart; I just called her Dot – that was my endearment. I don't think I've ever called her Dorothy, some of her friends have but she's just Dot to me and that's the way I like it and she was the same with me. 'Jim' didn't ever have a sweetheart or darling attached because I don't believe in that. She couldn't have been more wonderful.

Having five children with Dot was a blessing. My first was Valerie. I can't remember how old she was before I went abroad but she must have been about three and a half years old when I came home. She was an agile little thing and could turn her body inside out. Talk about double-jointed, I'd never seen anything like it.

Anyhow going back to my wife, she used to keep us all spotlessly clean. At times she'd have eight shirts to iron for the boys. I hated ironing shirts, sometimes she'd have so much washing and ironing, it's no wonder I took the children out so much on my own, she never had the time, always too busy in the house doing the things because we didn't have the luxury of today's modern appliances like vacuum cleaners, dishwashers or automatic washing machines. We did however have a twin tub from Hoover but that's all that helped her with the washing.

Whenever we went out as a family, Dorothy would be in the front the five children following behind her and me behind them to make sure the children didn't get lost or wander away. I can remember how well groomed we all were, with our clothes spotlessly clean, our hair well combed to such a degree that on many occasion we were complemented. Many people have said to us, "What a lovely family you've got."

We travelled everywhere on the bus or the trains and I just can't explain how good the good times were. Even going back to our wedding day, it was a bit unique when we sang our song, 'Apple Blossom Time'. What more can I say other than I wouldn't ever get another Dorothy like her, wouldn't matter where I tried, or how I tried, or for how long. I will love her all my life and I will never love anyone else because there's no one else like her.

See next page for two early family photographs. Firstly with (from l to r and back to front) Jim, Valerie, Dorothy, Dad with Phillip, Mother with Daryll, Michael and Christopher. Secondly, Jim with Daryll, Dorothy with Phillip, Michael, Valerie and Christopher.

****

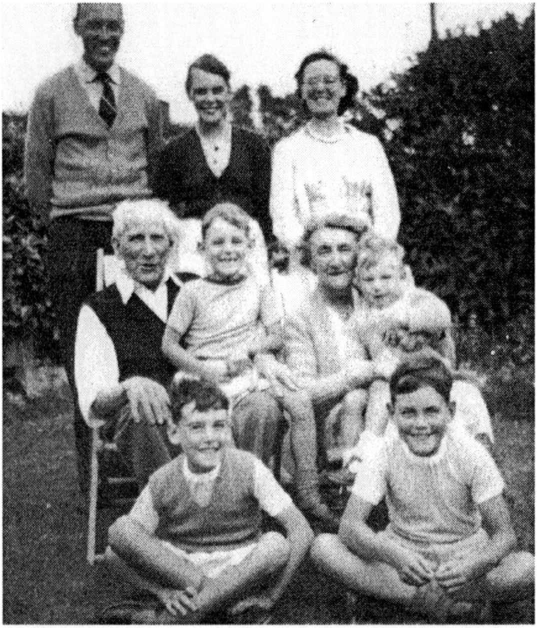

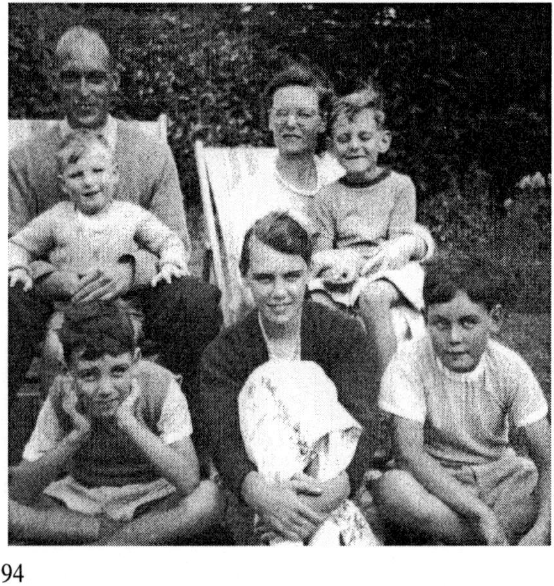

Now I'm going to talk about my children, the eldest of which is my daughter Valerie. Right from when she was a little girl she was a born acrobat and dancer. At the age of four, she was doing ballet and was able to do every sort of dance you could imagine – she only had to be shown once. It's my greatest regret that when Valerie was in her prime, probably when she was about twelve, we could not afford to send her to a proper drama or ballet school. I have no doubt at all in my mind she would have been a great success if we'd only had the money. I think we missed out on that opportunity; she would have been a great professional dancer. My poor Valerie, she has had so much bad luck you could not imagine.

Valerie was very good at school and before leaving school, she took up teaching adults to ballroom dance. She used to go to Ken Shouler's dance in Crawley. Ken Shouler's used to teach Valerie to dance and at the early age of twelve years Valerie was already teaching adults to dance with him. Valerie won loads of medals for dancing that she had to pass each time with every dance. It didn't matter what dance it was, Valerie would pick it up in minutes. I remember when they first brought out the new dance, I forget what it's called now, Valerie only had to see it once and she got it, her friend as well was the same as Valerie, very quick at learning.

Valerie married Bill and had a son they named Paul.

Paul was a wonderful little thing. He had learnt to open the boot of our cars from the early age of three. He was simply amazing. His dad and I always knew what he was after. He'd open the boots and fetch a golf club. He just had to have a swing with the golf club. All he did when he got hold of a club was practice his swing.

He was only little, in fact the golf club was almost as tall as Paul was. Paul followed his passion and went on concentrating on his swing for years. When he was twelve he was selected to represent England in the tournament for boys up to sixteen years of age. Paul had his Great Britain uniform; he was very smart in that, he thoroughly deserved it because he was brilliant.

I still remember when I used to take Paul to music lessons. I'd take him in my car and he'd sit in the front seat with me, proud as punch with his school uniform still on and he'd have his trombone case by his side. He'd sit there with this sweet smile of pride that matched my own, both of us, our chests swollen with a love only we understood. They were magical moments. Paul knew I loved him dearly.

At the early age of twenty-two or twenty-three, he held the course record in Sussex. He was known in every golf course in Sussex. Paul was a member of Cottesmore Golf Club on the Horsham Road. The Cottesmore Club had a huge photograph of Paul above the stairs to the clubroom. He was a loyal member.

Paul was young and very near to marriage to his girlfriend Charlotte. They'd been together for many years. Charlotte (nicknamed Lotty) and her mother decided to move house. On the day of the move, Paul helped Lotty and her mother. At the end of the day, Paul was exhausted as was Lotty and her mother. It was late and Charlotte's mother asked Paul if he'd stay the night since he'd worked so hard. That evening, exhausted and totally drained, Paul and Lotty retired to bed. In the morning Lotty's mother called out as they both seemed to have slept quite long hours and there had been no response from them the first few times she had called out. She wondered why Paul and Lotty didn't stir, so she went into the bedroom and to her horror found them both dead.

Paul lay across the middle of the bed where he'd apparently tried to get out. He must have collapsed. Lotty was in the normal position lying in bed but dead. What happened that night would not have happened again in a thousand years, for people had been living in that house before Charlotte and her mother moved in and they never did get carbon monoxide poisoning. Sadly for Paul and Lotty, it was a case of wrong place, wrong time. The wind, fumes and weather conditions seemed to have crept in like a thief at night to steal their sweet lives as they became overwhelmed by the poisonous gases that came in from the boiler not serviced for years. Both died of carbon monoxide poisoning. It took the police several days before they could tell us their cause of death. That was a terrible ordeal, a very terrible ordeal especially for Val and Bill her husband. Paul was their only child.

I knew Bill so well, I had taught him as a youngster, and he wanted to become a computer programmer. He'd sit with me at my desk in A.P.V. and learn a bit about accounting. Learning accounting would have been useful to him as a potential programmer. I didn't know that I was coaching my prospective son-in-law.

Valerie had come home one day and announced that she wanted to bring her boyfriend home to meet us. I remember opening the door to Bill. I was very surprised; my Valerie had brought home the very man who I had coached. I hadn't been aware that the two of them were courting. What a small world! Bill always called me Jim, never Dad. I liked him calling me Jim he was a wonderful guy.

Paul had been unfortunate to have lost his life. He had already gone through all of the handicaps and turned professional before he died. Great prospects lay ahead of him had he lived. We all expected him to go to high places

We had had our Fiftieth wedding anniversary just before Paul died. He had given us some little things we treasure very much which my wife keeps in her china cabinet where she lives now.

He was such a lovely boy, a grandson to be proud of!

Paul would have loved his Uncle Christopher's villa in Portugal which backed onto an incredible golf course, but sadly he didn't get to go there.

Christopher owned a remarkable villa in a place called Quinto do Lago in Portugal, the type of villa that competes with the likes of Cliff Richard and Madonna who were in fact his neighbours a few acres down the road. Christopher lived at his villa. The villa had all the trappings of wealth and splendour, swimming pool, Jacuzzi, tennis courts, attached to an exclusive golf course. It was fabulous.

I didn't swim when I visited, I just pottered about in my shorts. We were out there on summer vacation. Bill, Val's husband, myself and a few others. He was on his way to the Jacuzzi and invited me to join him. I followed him and when we got to the water, he was stepping on stones that were partly out of the water, quite big ones.

He was jumping from one to the other and I trailed right behind him when suddenly he stepped on a slippery one and went down BANG onto the floor. I don't really remember much after that only that I knew he had cut his head open. It all happened so quickly and I hardly remember who came over to help us. I simply cannot remember a thing besides seeing poor Bill lying on the floor. I'm sure he was bleeding.

Poor Val, she eventually took him to the hospital in Albufeira in the Algarve. When we got to the hospital, it was so serious that she had to get an air ambulance privately purchased by herself to fly him back to England from Portugal. He came in on an air ambulance and went into St Catherine's hospice in Crawley. We found out that Bill had cancer and Val sat vigilantly at his side for approximately six months while he was slowly dying from cancer.

I just cannot believe two tragic accidents could happen to the same person in one lifetime. Whatever had she done to deserve all that? I do think sometimes all my prayers weren't answered, but then sometimes Jesus needs angels and reaches out for them and Paul and Bill were two angels called on duty.

Fortunately Val met a partner who's been very good to her, he's one of the most wonderful drivers I've ever driven with. It doesn't matter how much you talk to Bill whilst he's driving, he's never distracted. He will never take his eyes off the road, never. I feel as safe as houses when I'm with Bill, he's one of the finest drivers I've ever driven with and I have complete confidence in him taking Val out and I know he's made her very happy despite all the troubles. After all who could expect her to live alone after all that she's been through. Poor Val, my princess, she's now sixty-five, you would not believe it if you saw her she looks ten or twelve years younger than that, always well groomed just as my Dot had taught her back in her day.

Bill, Val's partner used to be a professional

caddy seen many times on television. He caddied for some of the most important professionals. Bill knew his golf like no other and he was highly regarded in his profession. He travelled all over the world and after he retired he played socially.

Bill is a wonderful man and has paid tribute to the memory of Val's first husband Bill and her son Paul by creating a wonderful memorial in their honour at Cottesmore Club. Val is a member of Boardhill Club and I think she is also a shareholder. It's a nine hole course for folk who don't want to play eighteen holes. It's a proper course with bunkers and all the hazards you find on a normal course. It has its own driving range and a lovely club house where you can socialise after playing your round of golf.

I've been there a couple of times and I loved the atmosphere and good food. Val also planted a tree as a memorial to her husband and son. She's done a lot of work and extended it to include a private area where you can be taught by a professional golfer. It's quite an amazing set-up and there are even three monitors that record your lesson which you can watch afterwards to go over your moves and the tutor can discuss it with you. This has all been made possible by Val and she is really committed to this cause in memory of her family.

Every year, Val holds an annual prize giving and she has the wonderful support of her partner Bill. It's quite a while since I've been there but I know they still do it.

****

Christopher! My son, the 'go getter.' When he was about five years old he would be up in the morning at Campbell Road and go to the spot where his grandfather had been digging the night before and continue the dig. Christopher never took to a child's spade, he had a proper spade, a small one, but a proper spade – It was his height. He loved helping his grandfather dig the plot. He would rise early in the morning and get to digging where granddad had left off. What a trooper! Whether or not he was a successful digger, that I can't testify, but his enthusiasm was paramount.

At the age of twelve he asked permission to do a paper round. Dorothy and I gave him our blessings, provided he be careful and vigilant out there as back in those days it was unsafe for boys and girls to do paper rounds.

My father-in-law and I were busy concrete coping outside 25 Campbell Road one day. At the time Christopher was maybe two or three years old. They brought him out wrapped in a red blanket. He was heading for the isolation hospital in Croydon. They thought he'd got meningitis. In those days meningitis was a killer and we could not believe it. Both my old father-in-law and I wept as we watch him being taken away. A little boy in this red blanket into the isolation hospital where we could not go and see him, we just had to sit and wait. We eventually got a call from the hospital, it was good news, he had not contracted meningitis and we were allowed to collect him. Collecting him was a memorable day. As we walked up this long garden path to the hospital I could see this little chubby figure, with his nose pushed against the glass. I nudged Dot, – "I think I can see a little boy with his nose pushed against the glass." We got further along the road and he was going absolutely mad, and yes he did have his little nose pushed against the glass and as fat as anything. This little two year old, maybe three, was kicking, struggling and laughing uncontrollably. It was our little Christopher who had recognised us as we walked towards the hospital. He got more and more excited as we drew closer. He was dressed in a lovely little blue velvet suit which my wife bought him. The joy on that boy's face is as fresh in my memory today as if it were yesterday – Unforgettable!

Now all my boys were the same, they all worked very, very hard in the garden. On the one side of the allotment, Valerie had her own little vegetable patch and a little flower patch where she'd grow her own seeds, so she'd often go with us to the allotment to tend to her patch. The kids loved going to the allotment although I never really summoned their help. All of them would want to dig and muck about with the mud except for Philip. He'd stand and watch but never get his hands dirty, though he'd know what was going on.

Christopher did his paper round diligently and would also work for Mr Jones the butcher on

Saturdays, helping him in the shop. I thought it was good experience for him to be out there doing things for himself so I never discouraged him. None of my other children thought about doing paper rounds, not that they had to or I expected them to, it's just that Christopher wanted to and was a keen learner. This went on for some time and I thought it was time for Christopher to jump ship to something more substantial. Since I had worked at the airport continuously for two years, by which time Christopher was twenty-one – I thought it would be a good idea to try to get him an airport job. With this, I asked him if he would be interested in an airport job to which he replied "YES."

I managed to find a position for Christopher and he came to work at the airport with me. As I mentioned before, he was a keen young man willing to do anything and wanting to perfect everything. Eagle-eyed and lion-hearted, he sponged up information and executed tasks with ease and precision. It made me proud to watch my son go from strength to strength. There was no doubt in my mind of this young man's capabilities. He learnt everything about the industry. An achiever, that's my Chris.

Chris retired in 1998. He came, he saw, he conquered. But there's more, much more to my Chris. Money and good fortune were not what Chris was all about – Yes, we can all agree that Christopher was a man of great wealth and a fabulous success story. Today I look at my son and know in my heart that his success came to him for good reason. God knew his heart. I remember praying for my children, I'd pray that they'd be blessed with wisdom and knowledge that would help them lead a life of goodness. I'd pray that they would be blessed with vision and strength and that they would learn compassion and humility. Today I sit and know that my prayers were heard. I see what my children have achieved as individuals as they all have their own little success stories. In conclusion it is my firm belief that Christopher's wealth is not the silver lining – The silver lining is his heart and his immense generosity that outlines the true Christopher – his ability to give, to share, to embrace and to include those of lesser fortune in his world of love and goodwill. I want my son to know that I appreciate and love what he stands for and hope that the rest of my family feel equally happy and appreciative of this wonderful pillar of strength that stands amongst us, watching, guarding and looking out for all. Let us not ponder on material wealth – I want all to know that the blessing of wisdom, vision, compassion and humility are the gifts that life donates to those who readily embrace them and that is how I see my Christopher. Someone who embraced life's gifts then gave back in return.

****

Let me move on to my other son Michael. Now Michael was a dashing young boy with curly jet-black hair and an infectious smile. I might be guilty of fatherly pride, but if I tell you that Michael's ability to bring laughter and joy to people and situations is by no means an exaggeration. The boy simply had a wonderful personality and sense of humour that would leave us all in stitches of laughter. I ask myself over and over, was it that cheeky face and charming smile of his that would make people want to tease out even more cheek and end up rolling with delighted laughter. What pride I'd feel observing those moments.

I remember the time we went to the hall of mirrors where you stand in front of different mirrors that make you look thin, fat, distorted and loads of other disfigured images. Michael was a right clown the whole time. We laughed more at him than at our distorted images – it was such a hilarious occasion.

Well, this funny boy grew up and grow up he did. I would describe him as a bit of a lad, charming the girls and all with his smile, wit and humour. When he was twelve, bit of an early starter, he met a lovely young lass called Tessa. I never did get to ask how they met, since Tessa went to a Catholic school and Michael attended a local school close to home. We got to meet Tessa's parents whom I thought were wonderful people. Sadly for Michael, the family had to move to North Wales to an island. Unfortunately we didn't get to see them much, but over the distance and years, Michael and Tessa did keep in contact and ended up marrying each other. I got to sample my daughter-in-law Tessa's wonderful cooking. I remember she'd make pastry dishes that would melt in your mouth, just like the pastries Dot would make. She was a really wonderful cook and I loved it when she'd make me Christmas cake, sausage rolls and milk tart. That was my treat every Christmas and I looked forward to it.

Michael and Tessa enjoy what I consider to be a marriage solid as a rock. They have a beautiful home which is kept spotlessly clean by Tessa who is terribly house-proud. They have a daughter called Sarah and she too keeps her house spotlessly clean for her son Adam. Just like her mum Tessa. Sarah has a son called Adam; he is my first great-grandson. Adam is Sarah's only child; he's a lovely little boy, full of affection and laughter and has a lovely speaking voice. It brings me joy when I hear Adam speak or chuckle. Everyone thinks the world of him – who wouldn't – his sweet voice is like music to the ears and we all love it when he gets chatting. So there they are; Michael, Tessa, Sarah and Adam – the joy they bring to my heart is knowing that their family is so united, steady and wholesome.

In today's world of free speech, poor communication and loss of respect among couples, it's difficult to find such solid marriages as that of Michael and Tessa's. Seems sad when the trust in a marriage takes flight, it doesn't often find its way back and the children suffer the consequences. I will shelve this thought immediately, as it does not apply to my Michael and Tessa.

****

Now Phillip is another story. Phillip is the son that didn't like to get his hands dirty when we were out in the garden. He would stand at the patio door and watch from a distance and although he wouldn't participate in the shovelling or planting, he wouldn't miss a trick and made sure he knew what was going on. He was the academic, he'd sooner write the instruction manual on how to dig and plant than actually muddy up his wee hands. Phillip, true to his character turned out to be 'the academic'. He was a very clever lad indeed and outshone his peers at the local school he attended and was awarded a scholarship.

If you think I was proud, double that and times it by one hundred and then you'll know how I felt. My boy did himself justice, I was right about Phillip, and not all was in vain. He certainly added pride-height to my slight frame. I can clearly recall the days of how he refrained from our family garden digging festivities and my thoughts at the time that he'd be fine and that I had nothing to worry about – not everyone enjoys wrestling with mud and weeds I thought – he'd be good at something else.

Phillip went on the complete his education at a Grammar school in Crawley. He proved to be an exceptional student and rose to great heights.

When he left school he went to work for Sun Alliance based in Horsham. Naturally Phillip, still a young man in early employment, started at the bottom of the ladder. He was ambitious and inquisitive, always in top form and on the look out for greater prospects and opportunity. His day would come for him to take flight. He enjoyed his job at Sun Alliance and so it came to pass when one day he saw a notice appealing for volunteers to work at their offices in Australia. Phillip saw this as an opportunity and seized upon it, volunteering to emigrate. I remember the day he left, it was a sad and happy moment but I knew he was moving on to greater things and that was his blessing.

Phillip gradually climbed the corporate ladder and became one of the chief officers in the computer department. He enjoyed much success in his career and lifestyle except for the time when he and his wife Shirley ended their marriage. They have a daughter called Sally-Anne; she's my second eldest grandchild. Sally-Anne came to live in England and married Stuart, a construction engineer. I am a proud great-granddad to their lovely little daughter Ruby. She's my second great-grandchild and Adam is my first.

Sally-Anne visits me on occasion. She's a lovely young lady with as much promise as her dad. I was so delighted the day she brought little Ruby over and I was able to cradle her in my arms.

I've had photographs taken with Ruby in my

arms. She is simply adorable. The day I held her I could feel her little legs kicking away at me and I thought she was getting so excited, I could see her cheeks moving and it was wonderful holding her. I remember saying to Sally-Anne, "Look at her kicking at me getting all excited." Sally-Anne delighted me when she said, "She's trying to smile at you Granddad." I said, "Aww is she?" I couldn't see, bless her little heart.

Phillip did marry again and although his marriage to Shirley did not work out, they still kept in contact. Shirley met Phillip's new wife Susan and maintains a friendship with them both. I guess this may seem an unusual situation, but it's one that shows how respect for each other's needs can be simplified by being civil toward one another. Civility, one of life's great skills

Phillip and Susan had two children, Melanie and Ben. Both went to university in Australia. Melanie has also been to Japan and speaks fluent Japanese and Ben works in a hi-fi equipment shop.

Susan's parents used to own one of the biggest electrical shops in Sydney. I understand from general talk that the family business was about forty years old and has now been handed down to the eldest daughter.

****

There's that famous old saying that brings to mind my son Daryll. Those who make things happen, those who participate in things that happen, and those who watch things happen. Daryll was the glorious maker and participator. He'd stop at nothing. Daryll is talented and extremely precise when he does anything. He is never frazzled by challenge or change. He possesses this wonderful personality of warmth and generosity. He is sensitive and compassionate and has all the makings of a man of standing and amazing character.

Unfortunately for Daryll, given the advancements in my own career and various circumstances, we got to move house and town fairly often – twelve times in thirty years if I recall correctly. Daryll being the youngest suffered the most in terms of constant change as each time when he'd just settled into a job, we'd have to move.

Daryll's first job was working in a foundry working with heavy-duty material. He became friendly with his foreman Eddy and every Friday and Saturday the two of them would go out clubbing with two girls from their workplace. I think that this was a moment in life that Daryll really enjoyed as they did this for a good five years.

Unfortunately, we continued to shift house and town and Daryll would move with us. I do say that despite constant upheaval, Daryll remained resilient and he would be the best at what ever he set out to do no matter where he was. In fact, Daryll is the best DIY man I know.

He would help me with all the fixtures and fitting whenever we moved house, putting up curtain railings, hanging up picture frames, drilling and fixing broken cupboards, the lot – he was a superb handyman.

I remember at one of our many stopover towns, Daryll got a job as a carer in an old-age home. He must have witnessed many terrible situations and had to do some unsightly jobs that many people would find unbearable, but Daryll being the compassionate and caring person he is, didn't mind and helped effortlessly in the old people's home.

It is unfortunate that from the early age of twelve, Daryll suffered from severe back ache. Daryll has a twisted spine which cannot be corrected, so he will always suffer. As much as he tried not to cause us concern, we were always aware of the pain he'd endured and how he'd bravely champion on despite his moments of discomfort. He'd try not to raise alarm when his back would give way and he'd discreetly adjust his posture in order to alleviate his pain. I remember one time we were lifting slabs, Daryll hurt his back and collapsed – when he got up, he looked at me and told me he was fine and could carry on. Daryll would carry on working despite the odds and it would hurt me to see my son going through all this and I could do nothing to ease his pain.

I knew the agony Daryll went through and

I know how he soldiered on. Going out for a meal to a restaurant was uncomfortable, almost unbearable for him because he would have to stand up several times to reset his back. I think the world of my son Daryll and love him dearly. He excelled in all the things he did and many benefited from his kind nature. He's retired now and enjoys his hobby of photography. Fortunately he doesn't have to worry about working anymore. His brother Christopher has taken care to ensure that Daryll is comfortable. Daryll has nothing to worry about nowadays, why should he. He deserves the generosity and comfort.

6

LIFE'S CHALLENGES

I'd like to talk a bit about myself, the challenges I faced and how I overcame them. It was a moment in life I seemed to have lost touch with. I suddenly arrived at a time in my life where the world seemed to have stopped and nudged me in a way that indicated that this was my cue to jump off. I experienced this moment a few times before I was jostled back into the world that gave value, significance and a reason to keep going. Today I sit happily doing what I love most. Listening to my music and writing my book.

I think back to the time when my mother told me I should pray to Jesus and that he would take care of me. I always prayed, then my family arrived and I started to pray for them too. Perhaps I had stopped praying for me because I felt I was giving Jesus too much work, but the day I was reunited with my vision for life, I realised that no task was too big for Jesus and that in fact I was blessed and more – I just had to reach out and appreciate it and give thanks. It was a difficult journey. The moments of doubt hindered progress, feelings of anxiety suffocated my desire to live, and the fear of rejection tugged at the core of my heart in a way difficult to express.

Having gone through my life, I have fond memories. I recall starting off with the great love and affection from my parents, becoming a teenager and successfully finding odd jobs. I remember enlisting to join the RAF and being accepted even though everyone doubted I'd be accepted. Then there was the war, not such a great experience, but I emerged unscathed. I remember meeting my wonderful wife and the joy of the arrival of each child. Of course my personal achievements were many.

So why then did I sink into depression in 1997? Was it perhaps because my mother and sister suffered from depression that depression was determined not to exclude me? I don't know, all I can say is that this journey was treacherous and I needed to find a way out. Sadly depression did not overlook my son Daryll or my daughter Valerie. They too have been at the mercy of that dreadful state of being. We must agree then that it's a genetic disorder.

In 1997 a year before my son retired I became very ill, I had a breakdown. I couldn't even play my music and that was the early signs that things were bad. I couldn't bear to listen to music in my own private music room.

At the time my daughter-in-law Irene and my son Christopher suggested I went to a clinic in Typhurst under the observation of Dr Paul Gwimmer. Dr Gwimmer had a surgery in Harley Street. He was a very well-known and highly-regarded psychiatrist. I was admitted into this beautiful clinic in Typhurst, a home for people with depression. The treatment was financed by Christopher and Eileen. I was in a terrible state. I kept wondering how this could have happened to me after all my years as one who undertook great feats of responsibility all his life. Nothing had ever worried me in the past – I had been capable, able and even sought after. Beside all that, I had retired in 1978, this was 1997, almost twenty years later and the big 'D' (depression) hit me like a hammer to a nail.

I recall little about that first depression attack; all I do remember was that I had stopped talking. Dr Paul Gwimmer took care of me and I had to be given ECT (Electroconvulsive Therapy). This therapy is administered to get your brain moving and jerk you back into life. I would be wheeled into the ECT room and put to sleep. The attachments would be fitted around my head and the therapy administered. I had six sessions of the ECT treatment which seemed to have worked, as I seemed to have regained a spring in my step and started to listen to my music again.

In 1998 I had another serious breakdown. This time I went into the Priory Clinic in Hove. I paid for the treatment. Unfortunately, this time I had a complete breakdown. I was taken care of by a young psychiatrist. He used various techniques to assist my recovery especially since I had been taking a vast concoction of tablets.

The one technique he taught me was the art of relaxation and meditation which I still use today. This was the most significant part of my treatment. He taught me how to eliminate everything from my head and how to journey to my place of solitude, peace and calm. This was a total shutdown technique that would allow me to take myself to a place and time that gave me joy. One of my visualisations is a walk along the Thames tow path in Kingston toward Hampton Court where there's the lovely River Thames lined with boats and steamers, people waving at me and I'm waving back. The birds are chirping, the ducks are quacking. It's a glorious day and an enjoyable walk along the Thames from Kingston to Hampton Court.

This is the place my mother and father often took me – they were happy times. My other favourite memory hence visualisation is Wakehurst Place, home of the Royal Society of Horticulture where they experiment with seeds from all over the world. Wakehurst has this wonderful building that I loved to look at. It has absolutely beautiful ponds. I call them lakes. You go from one lake to the other then onwards to the next. The walk is a long way, and you have to make sure you're walking the right way; otherwise you lose yourself and finish up where you started. These are my two favourite places I visit when I meditate. It took the young psychiatrist some time to teach me this technique and now I am even able to go into meditation when I'm surrounded by people. I don't need to be alone in my room and I sometimes take a quick two-minute excursion.

I was discharged from the Priory, but it wasn't long after that when I suffered another breakdown. When I returned to the Priory Clinic, they only had doctors qualified to treat alcoholics and drug addicts. At the time of my return, they did not have a psychiatrist to treat my condition.

They eventually commissioned a doctor from Worthing to treat me. He would come in every day to monitor my progress. He put me on a tablet called Lithium, a very strong antidepressant. I had already been taking a cocktail of other antidepressant tablets as well as tranquilisers. Lithium was additional and the doctor informed me that it was a very, very strong class of drug. The benefit was if all else failed, i.e. the other cocktail of tablets I was on, Lithium would take charge and do the work which the other tablets failed to do. In short, Lithium was the drug that would kick me back into life and had to be administered under strict supervision.

That was my last manic breakdown, a time when I lost all and almost took my own life. It had been by far the worst attack, because I had to be fed and only in my room. My diet at the time was milk drinks and sometimes I'd eat a sandwich.

I remember vaguely the night I almost took my life. I went to bed one night, no thoughts, no feeling, and no sense of anything. I went to bed normally. I kept a bottle of aspirin in my drawer that I used to take for a headache occasionally. I'd get headaches sometimes when I listened to my music with headphones. They were never serious. The aspirin would do the trick.

This particular night I suddenly woke up, I don't know what time it was, but it was early morning and dark. I was suddenly overwhelmed with this great depression. I felt my will to go on living leave my body and I knew that I had to pray to Jesus to thank him for the wonderful life he had given me and to pray that my wife would understand that I had lost control of my desire to go on living.

This night, I was determined to die. A quick recollection of my life reeled through my head as I carefully prepared groups of five lots of tablets. For the first time, I was in control and knew what I wanted. I wanted to die and I had the means. Images of my past flashed in to my head giving me reason as to why I should end my life. I was scrapped in the air force, I no longer had the responsibility of a job, music started to give me headaches. I was never an idle man and now I was idle, the flashes were fast and furious confirming that ending my life was the thing to do.

I quickly prayed for forgiveness and threw the tablets down – although it was a decisive decision, I felt a pang of regret for I knew my actions would hurt my loved ones and that they wouldn't understand the immense depression I felt as I took those tablets. I drifted into delirium and then finally passed out. My wife found me in the morning which wasn't too late, because I lived to tell the story.

I honestly had meant to die. It wasn't a wake-up call, I simply had no will to live. I was picked up from the hospital by my son-in-law Bill and all the rest of the family except the ones who lived abroad. Bill wheeled me out of the hospital and I remember cursing all the way along until we got down to the reception area in the Princess Royal Hospital in Haywards Heath. I was saying to myself, "Why have I not died, what the hell have I got to do to die?" And then when we got to the reception area they started buying cakes and tea and we were having a joke. I thought to myself, "My goodness me, what a fool I was to think I would never have experienced all this if I had died!"

I will never ever do that again, never! I regret everything I've done – I will never ever get into that state again because I know what caused it. I suppose I can say I was lonely, but I don't know how I got into that state. I never sat about dreaming after that.

Christmas Eve 2004 we had carers coming in to help me and to help my wife. One of the carers said to my wife and me, "Jim whatever's the matter with you, you're beginning to shake." By the evening I was shaking more and by the time I went to bed my head was shaking, my arms were shaking, my legs were shaking and I thought, I'm never going to get to sleep. I did go to sleep and in the morning I didn't know anything, I was in a coma.

When this coma came on, my wife and the children did not know what to do, it was Christmas Day, Christmas morning, I was unconscious in a coma and they were faced with either sending for an ambulance or trying to give up the Christmas lunch the family had planned. They apparently thought they would take a chance and leave me and try to keep me safe during Christmas. I think it was my Michael that carried me on his shoulder like a sack of coal; I don't know how he did it because I was heavy. He got me out of the lounge and into the dining room. How he got me into a chair I'll never know. I sat there apparently and ate my dinner, my two sons fed me with a spoon and they said I ate everything, mince pies, Christmas pudding, everything they offered me, I ate. In the end they thought it best not to feed me anymore as I'd possibly lost my senses and would carry on eating because I wasn't well enough to understand that I was full.

The following day I was rushed into a private nursing home in Goff's Park. I have a faint remembrance of being interviewed by a doctor, but my thoughts were and still are that I was in a huge ground, like a football ground but I know in my mind that there's nowhere like that in Crawley. I was under the impression that I was standing at a table with my wife and the doctor. According to my wife he was questioning me on all sorts of things to establish whether I was a mental case or a normal hospital case. Fortunately I was diagnosed normal, and luckily not a mental case, as had I been diagnosed as having a mental breakdown, it would have been marked on my record for life. They evidently found I was not a mental patient and he put me into Goff's Park private nursing home.

I experienced the most horrible withdrawal effects which I will not talk about to anybody, I don't know if any of them were true but I imagined that I was in a big cot with the locked sides and I could not get out. This is probably a complete fantasy. I was probably sitting in a bed being fed. I don't remember anything at all while I was in this coma. I was so ill that the family were told there was every chance I may never come out of it. Not all the family were there as some were abroad when the doctors told them what the worse case scenario was.

I think they were more worried as to whether I was going to live or die. The doctors told me that I was very, very close to death. They had said that if I came out of the coma it did not mean I was finished or on the road to recovery. There was a likelihood that I would relapse back in to the coma and never come out of it. The tablets had caused me an awful lot of trouble but then again I suppose it's the price I paid for a mistake or misjudgement that anyone else is capable of making.

I've separated from my wife not for any other reason than it's just a peculiarity. When I came out of this coma I was lying on a lounger all day, my wife was so worried about me she was afraid of me doing anything in case I hurt myself. I'd lost my balance, so I had to use a zimmer frame because I could not walk properly, I could only do a few yards and then I had to walk back. She used to come with me time after time, I'd have a little walk round the garden because I couldn't do very much, I just lost my balance.

One night I phoned up Christopher and asked him to come to see me. I needed to talk to him. Christopher came home that weekend arriving on a Friday night. He came up to my music room, I said to him, "Chris, for God's sake get me out of this house. I don't know what it is but I can't leave Mum to have all this worry. It's not right; it's not fair to her. I'd much rather go into a home. I'm hoping you'll find me one."

7

ANECDOTES FROM MY LIFE

My Teeth

As you will have read, as a boy, I was very weak and had been kept from school for the first ten years of my life. I had many ailments as a growing child and into my adulthood. I just never caused alarm about any of them as I didn't want my family to be overly concerned. One of my most severe conditions was my teeth. I suffered endlessly and they were the cause of a lot of other aches and pains as I grew up.

When I was about eight or nine, I used to suffer with terrible earache. My mother would take me to the doctor to have my ears syringed, but nothing would come out and I'd still have this excruciating earache. There were times it was so bad, I would bang my head on the wall, and then I'd sit there with a headache as well, because I'd be banging my head against a brick wall and not plasterboard. I'd sit there and ask myself just how long could this pain go on for.

I eventually grew out of it. I was about sixty years old and suddenly I got severe toothache again. The pain was so agonizing it felt like an attack of the earaches I experienced as a youth.

I tried various methods and pressed hard on my tooth with cloves and whatever I could get my hands on to ease the pain. It was to no avail, the pain would not subside.

I grabbed the yellow pages and called a dentist. We lived in St Mary's Bay in Kent at the time. The dentist was in Hythe about eight miles from St Mary's Bay. When I got there I quite blankly without a hint of uncertainty ordered him to remove all my teeth. The dentist looked alarmed and asked why I seemed so resolute on removing all of them and not just the one that caused the pain.

My answer was simple. I was starting to get toothache and I didn't want to live with it. I had suffered as a child with severe earache and I did not want to suffer anymore. In fact I am now very sure that it was my teeth that had been the cause of my earache and headaches.

Over three separate appointments, the dentist extracted all my teeth. He told me that my teeth had severely damaged my gums and it was not possible for me to ever wear false teeth. He offered to take the impressions to construct a set of dentures for me but he seemed quite sure that I wouldn't be able to cope with them.

I didn't want to give up and although the dentist had expressed repeatedly that I'd be wasting my money, I insisted on giving it a go to wear false teeth. He took my gum impressions and ordered my false teeth.

I went in fairly confident and the dentist prepared to fit my dentures. He put the first half in. He had not even time to adjust them before I heaved and splattered. I was in such pain at just the touch of my gums that the dentist pushed back on his chair having quickly removed them.

"Mr Parker," he said, "you're not going to be able to wear these. I am really sorry, but your gums are too sensitive and damaged to hold the dentures in place and we can't have you heaving at the dinner table now can we?"

I begged with him, but he apologised and told me that it was just not possible because my gums could continue to recede for the following two to three months and not be suitable for dentures because they would be too flat. The length of my teeth had been abnormal and eroded my gums and I am now certain that my teeth had contributed to my earaches, particularly at the age of twelve when I was sprouting into adolescence.

My wife is witness to how hard I tried to be able to have a set of teeth so that when I ate I didn't nauseate others who sat at the table with me. But, it was just not possible, and I had to learn to cope in other ways without teeth.

****

Alec and Betty in St Mary's Bay

Dorothy and I lived in a quaint cottage in St Mary's Bay in Kent. We were very lucky to have wonderful neighbours, Alec and Betty. They had not been retired very long when we moved there. Alec was a first class green bowler, so he always dressed in his whites. He belonged to the New Romney Club.

He was a good man and Alec encouraged Daryll to join him in bowling. Daryll was always keen to try out new adventures, so he equipped himself with all the bowling paraphernalia and started to learn green bowling. He actually became really good at the sport and teamed with Alec and two of Alec's friends and played in the local championships and their team won a trophy.

As couples we made several trips up to Calais to take a ride to France and also to pick up a few duty-free goods. Alec used to enjoy his walks along the sea front from St Mary's Bay into Dymchurch and back. Dymchurch was really a seaside town for children, equipped with a mini amusement park. I on the other hand enjoyed going to New Romney on the other side and do a bit of fishing there. I'd catch eels, but daren't take them home with me because it made Dorothy queasy. Actually, Dorothy was afraid of snakes and she'd have nightmares about them even if she saw them on television and I believe that eels would have the same effect. The mere mention of a snake would send her reeling and writhing like one.

We were sitting in the lounge early one evening with Alec and Betty. Alec had been telling us what he was going to have for his supper that evening. He fancied some cheese, two pickled onions and a couple of biscuits, and then he'd watch a bit of telly and retire to bed. "Old habits die hard Alec," I had said, because this had been his routine since we'd met.

The following morning, our doorbell rang, nothing unusual, and Alec stood there with a large piece of pottery in his hand. He looked bewildered and spoke as if he didn't know me. "I've got this jug, does it belong to you?"

I called out to Dot, "Alec doesn't know me; he's brought a piece of china here."

"Alec, It's Dot," she said, but Alec continued to talk in a very meek voice.

"I don't know where this has got to go. I can't think where it's come from." He was in a totally different world. I don't know whether he had had an attack of dementia or even Alzheimer's but something serious had happened and after that he was taken away. Betty was left on her own. I think Alec died and Betty moved away. Sadly we lost touch with Betty.

****

Driving

In 1957 I applied for a driving licence, I did not have my own car but I learned to drive with a school motoring vehicle. I had booked twelve lessons. The day of my test, the examiner came out and instructed me to carry out standard manoeuvres. I was using a car that belonged to the driving school. After the standard manoeuvres, the examiner jumped into the car to test my road skills telling me where to go.

Turn left, I turned left, turn right, I turned right and as I did so, my door swung open. I quickly shut it, but unfortunately the incident made me fail my test. I didn't have a lot of money, but after that, I was determined to buy my own car, so I went down to the local dealership and bought my first car. I bought a Wolseley. I had to buy a car big enough to accommodate my family.

I decided to take on extra lessons with a man called Stan, a local caretaker at Sir Robin's Hall close to where we lived. Stan was passionate about American cars and he owned a Buick. He knew I failed my test and offered to give me lessons to help me pass at my next try. I eventually took the test and went home to five eager faces all waiting for me.

Barely time to open the door, I just about managed to squeeze into the entrance as they crowded around me. "Did you pass, Dad, did you pass?" The anxiety on their faces in anticipation of good news was very becoming. When they were little tots, the sound of their screeching excitement was music to my ears. Now they were a little older and they expressed their excitement differently, but still, they always brought joy to my heart.

I held my breath, taking in each expression of beady eyes staring at me. Dot had come out of the kitchen also keen to find out the verdict. "yyyyyyyyyes I passed." Then that good old sound of screeching excitement as they all sang "yeeeaaah" in unison.

"So, where would you like to go as your first trip in daddy's car?" I asked.

"Bognor Regis!" they yelled in harmony.

We packed a picnic basket, jumped into the car and we were off to Bognor Regis. All on board and we were on our way. We had to go up Bury Hill, which was really, really steep and a one way road. There was a lot of traffic, so we had to keep stopping. Unknown to me, this was having dire effects on my clutch and handbrake. It was not a new car and I didn't pay much money for it.

At one stage, we stopped and when I released my handbrake to pull off, I rolled back into the truck behind me. Ooops, I leaned out the window, but the driver of the truck shouted back for me not to worry as no damage had been done and signalled me to carry on.

The traffic was heavy and the start/stop traffic was taking its toll on my cheap car. My engine started to sieze and the splattering sounds were very threatening. People were staring as we jerked along the way. We eventually got to the top of Bury Hill where there was a policeman on point duty.

"Blimey, mate," he declared, "I sure did hear you coming. You'll need to get your car checked out; I don't think you're getting any further than this." He pointed me in the direction of the garage 200 yards from where we had parked.

The children were very disappointed and I was very worried. I didn't know how we were going to get back home. I rang up Stan and he kindly made his way up to Bury Hill to pick us all up in his Buick. Well, I was grateful to that big American Car that day and of course to our good friend Stan.

We didn't give up on our quest for adventures and we did go out as a family after we bought a decent car. One of our outings we particularly enjoyed was going on motor rallies. It was a type of treasure hunt and we'd be given a map to assist us finding the hidden objects. Phillip and Michael were brilliant map readers and we had lots of fun at this event.

I drove for forty years doing thousands of miles and was never once confronted by police. I never ever got a single endorsement on my licence. I packed up driving in year 2000 when I was registered partially blind, so now I use a taxi when I need to go somewhere.

****

Music and Food

Despite the absence of my teeth, I have to admit that it does not deter me from the types of food I eat. I love my food and I often go out looking for new pubs or restaurants to try out their menus. I can't see, but that's not a problem, because I usually pick the first thing on the menu. I'm not a fussy man; I'll eat anything and any cuisine in any part of the world.

I'm also very passionate about music. It's been food for my soul in many a difficult moment. I started to record music when the Beatles first emerged in 1966. I had always wondered what type of hobby would interest me when I eventually retired and since I enjoyed music so much, I guess this was destined to be my hobby.

I recorded my music on an old Toshiba reel-to-reel tape. I would tape about fifteen songs then play them back and select the ones I liked. There were usually only about three or four songs that I really liked. I carried on recording my favourite music until year 2000 just after I was registered partially blind. I had also stopped recording because after my coma my hands started to shake which made it difficult for me to press the record keys.

My favourite music is Motown and I also specialise in all pop music. I enjoy a bit of light classical music, as long as it doesn't last longer than fifteen minutes a piece. If I was to watch or listen to Beethoven's fifth symphony I would get bored after a quarter of an hour.

Two of the symphony films I'll never forget are *Dangerous Moonlight* and *The Third Man*. The piano music in those two films touched me so much; it brought tears to my eyes. Before I lost my sight, I used to use Windows 98 and adapted it to cater to my requirements. I had wanted to make a list of all artists by name like Diana Ross, Gladys Knight, etc. so that I could pull out every song of individual artists and listen to my hearts content.

I have ten thousand of my favourite songs which I have recorded myself. As I mentioned before, I am the biggest fan of Motown which I first heard in a record forty years ago when I first started recording in 1966.

I bought this record from a jumble sale at a school for one or two pence and I could not play it because it was so scratched. I tried for forty years to get a copy of that record till my granddaughter Lucy found a copy for me in Japan. That record is like gold dust to me, whenever I listen to it, it inspires me and helps me pass time.

It is gospel music sung by a beautiful gospel choir, a tribute to Berry Gordy to remember Tamla. Tamla was his wife's name and the records were all made in Motown which is a motor town of Detroit, so that is where Motown came from. The Motown tribute to Berry Gordy is a beautiful record. Perhaps you've got to be religious to like it as it is the Lord's Prayer sung. It's not everyone's choice of music, but I certainly do like it. Other great songs like 'Let it be' are sung by the great Diana Ross and Gladys Knight.

Stevie Wonder, Marvin Gaye, The Four Tops and The Temptations are all the greats I have enjoyed listening to. The CD costs me eight pounds but I took out insurance of one thousand pounds because I don't ever want to lose that CD. The music on this CD really inspires me. I have told matron that if ever I go off my food to get out that CD and play it to me. I also gave the matron a walkman with a mini cassette. I don't know what songs are on it but I do know that I like them all and I asked her to put that cassette in the coffin when I die because that is my wish.

****

My Dogs

When I was at RAF Melksham on my trade training, I was away for four weeks. The camp where I was based had three thousand men being trained at one time. We were all housed in huts holding twenty-four men. The huts were all identical, same windows, same doors, same steps, same everything. There were probably one hundred and twenty of these huts all in long rows.

During our free time, we were allowed to walk about the campus and socialise with chaps from other houses. I used to enjoy taking a walk to meet up with some of the lads and we'd just hang about. On a day, no different from the others, I went on my usual walk to my regular hang-out. When it was time to leave, I made my way back to my house and noticed that I was being followed by a Shepherd dog. I have no idea where the dog came from, but it just followed me.

She had a beautiful golden-brown coat with several layers of different shaded browns. Her coat was silky and smooth and she reminded me of Lassie from the TV programme.

The dog followed me for three weeks non-stop. When I'd go out training, she'd follow me and wait till I'd finish, then walk me back to my hut. Sometimes she'd go away, but each morning when I'd come out of my hut, the dog would be sitting there waiting for me. It was really strange, because she wouldn't react to any of the other lads, just me. Out of all the rows of huts that were identical, she'd always find my hut and sit out there. She never attempted to enter the hut; she'd just walk at my heel when I made my way to the training unit.

At the end of my training, I wasn't sure what to do. I didn't know whether to take her home with me or leave her behind. I eventually decided to take her home and made a make shiftcollar and lead. I had asked my dad to keep her whilst I was away and we did name her Lassie after all.

Lassie was generally an obedient dog and when I came home on leave, I'd take her out. One time I invited Dorothy to go on a boat ride with me along the Thames. We put Lassie on a lead and made our way to the Thames. We hired a boat and the ticket-master held the stern as Dorothy climbed in. I signalled to Lassie and she eagerly pounced in rocking the boat quite violently. Dorothy held steady, but her face was a bit white with the fear of toppling over into the water. I jumped in and we rowed downstream. Lassie sat gazing and every now and again yelping out with excitement as we'd row past other boats.

I turned to Dorothy and suggested a stopover at the next safety stop so that I could get out and stretch my legs and have a cigarette. Dot was ok with this and we stopped over, stretched our legs and I had my cigarette. We still had at least another half an hour of rowing before returning the boat to base.

Since it was only the two of us and no one to hold the stern whilst we got in, I briefed Dorothy on the best way to get in safely. She got in nicely, but then Lassie, full of doggy anticipation did what she did best and leapt into the boat with inexplicable enthusiasm. By this time, I had already released the rope from the safety post and the force of Lassie's jump pushed the boat out. Dot was screaming and Lassie sat oblivious to the panic she'd just caused. Dot had no paddle and shrieked with fear. It was a bit hilarious, because Lassie just seemed so pleased that she was in the boat. Dot's screams meant nothing to her. I guess I should have held the stern!

Fortunately enough one of the scullers pushed Dot back toward the safety post and we managed to eventually return the boat to the base. What an eventful afternoon it had been.

My second dog I owned was when I worked as a taxi driver. She was given to me by an elderly lady who knew me and asked if I could help her by taking care of the puppy. The puppy had a beautiful face with a white streak down her nose which made her very attractive. She was a beautiful jet black Labrador.

There I was left with a tiny puppy. I took her into my car and I was left contemplating on what to do with her. I knew Dorothy would not be very happy if I brought her home as the children kept her busy enough and she would not have time to look after the puppy as well.

Nevertheless, I decided to risk my bacon and take the pup home. It didn't take long for me to feel attached to this little bundle, she was lovely. I cautiously entered the house through the back door and as soon as the children saw her they went mad with excitement. Dorothy walked in and looked at me with an eye of disapproval. Just as that happened the puppy jumped up and began to greet everyone including Dorothy. I believe at that moment a bond was sealed. A silent agreement transpired between them and Dot ruffled her little head and went back into the kitchen.

We named her Trixie and she became very fond of Dot. My wife used to work part-time at the local newsagent across the road and she would return home in time for the children at around half past three. Trixie become so attached to Dot that she learned her routine. The neighbours would tell us how Trixie would come to the front door and look through the window panel exactly fifteen minutes before Dot was due home and wait.

They were baffled and joked saying that our dog could tell the time because her timing was so accurate when she'd exit to wait for Dot to return. Animals, especially dogs, are very intelligent and they do understand when they are loved.

We once took Trixie to the golf course to take a walk around the edges on the path, she was still very small but we took her off her lead because she was quite good and let her scurry off. The children and I were walking and eventually Valerie said to me, "Where's Trixie, Dad?" We all looked for her and I hoped that she hadn't gone far because if that was the case she would be out on the main road. Fortunately Valerie spotted her and tried to point her out to me. At first I could not see her but then I saw her little head pop up out of nowhere. She had fallen into a bunker and managed to scurry up the sides enough so that we could see her head. We eventually retrieved her and put her back on her leash.

8

WALSTEAD PLACE AND FRIENDS

On 13th August 2005 I asked my son to find me a home as I no longer wanted to burden Dorothy with my health problems. After all the problems that I had had and the way she had looked after me so well, I did not find it fair that she had to go through all that trouble again.

Christopher and my daughter Valerie apparently went through the yellow pages and picked out two homes. The following day, Valerie came to me and said that they had found two homes that were both very nice, except one was quite large and the other was smaller but quaint. I decided to visit the larger of the two first. We were greeted by a lovely bubbly carer. They were expecting me, because she already knew my name. I was very impressed with the entrance door. We were invited to be seated in the reception area to wait for the matron. I couldn't believe what I could see with the little sight I had left. There were lovely pictures on the wall and impressive high ceilings. I was convinced that this was a listed building. As you know, listed buildings are the 'Pride of Britain' controlled by a commission or heritage. Americans love to visit and take photos of British buildings that hold character and history. Owners of listed buildings are required to seek authorisation to make any minor alterations or restoration to their listed building.

We met with the matron, and I immediately liked her. Her voice was warm and friendly, calm and soft. She first showed me into the reception room which was equally as impressive as the waiting room with its high ceilings and chandeliers. We viewed the lounge which had about thirty easy chairs and scatter cushions. It was a bright airy room with a huge television set. It really presented an atmosphere of comfort. There weren't any sofas, all single armchairs that can be easily moved around when they have small group discussions or events.

Next we went into the Conservatory. Oh dear me, what a glorious moment as you enter. Sun-kissed spots and natural daylight reaching far and beyond to cover every angle. As you stand looking out at the vast lawns, you can almost touch nature. A beautiful room to experience unity with self and nature.

I was also showed the garden, which sadly I was unable to walk in, due to my imbalance, but it did captivate me when I saw it from the conservatory.

I then saw the dining room. The theme in this room was a melody of green and white with bursts of yellow from the daisies at each table setting. The character of this room seemed to have adopted a fragrant atmosphere from the natural colours of spring. This was a refreshing room with elegant table settings for four and fresh flowers.

Finally, matron showed me the room which was being offered to me. I couldn't believe my luck. It was on the first floor with a stairlift to help me go up to get to the corridor leading to my room from the social areas. I was told that this room is the biggest of the forty-five rooms in the whole building all of which are occupied by residents. That is an awful lot of people to cater for.

The proposed room that I was shown has a veranda which reaches out into the beautiful garden right in the middle of the country. I'm able to hear the birds sing if I rise early to listen to them start their day.

I immediately fell in love with the room as soon as I saw it. I really thought it would be a perfect place to live and I turned to my son to confirm my stamp of approval.

I can't fully explain my emotional experience at my first visit except that I felt the warmth in the voices that surrounded me and I knew that this is where I wanted to stay. I remember praying with conviction that my senses hadn't failed me and that my interpretation of the atmosphere was correct. Each and every room delivered its unique characteristic and inspiration. I prayed about this and I guess my family would be surprised about my commitment to my faith in Jesus, because I never spoke about religion to them. I used to feel too ignorant or guilty to talk about religion because I didn't really know much except what my mother told me.

My son paid for my accommodation at Walstead Place and on Wednesday 16th August 2005 at 11.00 a.m. only a few days after my visit, I moved in and I'm blissfully happy with my living conditions and the wonderful carers who surround me with love and attention.

Walstead Place has approximately eight men and thirty-five women residents. They're all beautifully groomed; all have their hair done regularly. Some of them are very old, two people over ninety-five and one nearing a hundred. All the ladies are nicely dressed with pretty skirts and dresses, all are a credit to the home.

Sometimes one of the residents may come into the dining room and one of the carers might notice one of the ladies with her bows tied unevenly and will put it right. If anyone is upset, they are always quick to give a cuddle or kiss whether it be a man or woman as everyone in the home has a loving nature.

I know all the staff at Walstead and I think they all work tirelessly. The gardener, who is responsible for the upkeep of the entire outside area, does a superb job especially when he trims the lawn creating the neat rows across its length. He also provides flowers for us all the year round so that our garden is never without flowers. I'm guessing that he has a greenhouse where he grows everything.

The first year I was at Walstead, he had planted a bed of every kind of dahlias about twenty-five feet long. I imagine that this can't be an easy task. I have no idea how he manages to do it all. I guess he's just one of those people who love what they do and also enjoy working with us old folk. He is always ready to help anyone.

Even the maintenance engineer has a star quality and is kind to us all. If something needs to be moved, he moves it; if it needs to be fixed, he fixes it. There's nothing he can't do. Our maintenance engineer and gardener work as a team helping each other. It's refreshing seeing people get on so well.

In the old days, the old folk would say, "A way to a man's heart is through his stomach." Well, I can tell you that our chef, who's a lady, has definitely reached my heart. I call her our wonder lady. Her pastries are superb and she bakes the most marvellous cakes.

No one goes unacknowledged if it's their birthday. All the staff come in led by the chef with a beautifully decorated cake and a few candles, to sing happy birthday and celebrate the moment. Most of them manage to blow out the candles with a little help from the chef or the matron. They really make you feel right at home, and we also get a glass of wine if we're up for it.

We also get to celebrate Valentine's Day in the dining room and we're each presented with a long-stem red rose wrapped in cellophane, just like the ones you would buy in Covent Garden. I don't think you even get that sort of treatment in some of the biggest hotels.

All this is organised by our wonderful matron. She works so hard and still finds time to entertain us and show love. She has a huge responsibility, managing the home and all the staff.

Matron is helped by the Administrations Officer whom I've seen surrounded by a pile of files she was sorting out. These ladies do work very hard, but their greatest skill is their efficiency and the ability to find time to share special moments with us.

Not forgetting deputy matron who also has the important job of overseeing many tasks. She's always friendly and approachable.

My laundry is taken care of by a very able and charming housemaid. Our laundry service is second to none. All our clothes are washed and our trousers pressed and cleaned. The carer fetches our laundry in the morning and it's returned the following morning beautifully ironed. It's a service comparable to no other, particularly for me since I mess my shirts often because I shake so much. I drop a lot of food on my shirts or trousers despite my serviette. Our laundry service delivers them back to me in pristine condition and stains removed.

I used to be allowed to wear a long red or black bib to protect my clothing, but matron sent out instructions disallowing us to wear them anymore.

I don't understand why they would have done this as I would have thought that they were made for people especially like me.

I really believe that Jesus sent me here. Walstead Place was mapped out for me and this is where I am happiest. I've tried to leave twice for reasons I felt were justified, but after talking to matron she did make me understand, and I realised that I had been wrong in my judgement. I guess I can put it down to old-age stubbornness, but you have to understand that we do have our moments.

I often sit and count my blessing and I experience frequent moments of appreciation for where I am today. I give thanks to Jesus for creating the opportunity for me to be surrounded by such beauty and love.

I am sure that I'm not the only one who feels happy in this home. It is hoped that other residents are aware of how lucky they are to be at Walstead Place. I will not accept a word of criticism about this home, the staff, the building or the food.

If I do hear anything negative, I tell people exactly what I think. I tell them to hush and I have no qualms about whether they like me or less. I've been treated well and the staff here are angels from heaven. I've already said that I have been sent here as my final resting place. I have no problem with the thought of death, but I have told people including the matron that I hope to live for another fifteen years, the reason being that both my parents died of natural causes at a very advanced age. So did my wife's parents so in our family lines there are no risks of strokes or heart attacks. The only thing would be that my mother suffered from depression as I do which is something I have already mentioned. I have however dealt with that and it will never happen to me again.

We also have a wonderful minibus driver who is married to the Administration Officer, and I believe he's been caring for people in one way or the other all his working life. He is patient and kind whenever he takes us out and has taken special care of me on a one-to-one basis. He doesn't only drive, but also provides support as a carer and happily helps serving tea, coffee and cakes. I love the way he always takes great care of me.

Two other people have been here at Walstead for a very long time. One is the senior carer who's been here for twenty years. Her name is on my door as my personal carer. The other lady who's been here too just under twenty years is one of the valuable members of the kitchen staff. She helps in the kitchen and serves the residents their tea and coffee delivering the perfect cuppa. We have five senior carers all capable of taking over roles and responsibility in the absence of matron.

I hope that I have not left anybody out as I've said they are all angels from heaven. I can't tell you how much I think of the matron as she has helped me so much and has allowed me to have whatever I have asked for in my room. I even have things to which she hadn't even agreed to, such as Sky which I have had put up twice. She could have said no, but she is wonderful in her cooperation.

Just one more story I'd like to share. When I first came here, after about two or three weeks, we were told that we were having an evening party. This party was being given in aid of the previous matron who left but was coming back this evening to be presented with a beautiful bouquet of flowers and a few gifts from the staff and residents.

I shook hands with the old matron and she greeted me kindly. After the flowers had been presented, the matron went around with a bottle in each hand one of red wine and the other of white wine.

An extraordinary thing happened to me whilst I sat there listening to all the cheer and chatter. A couple of carers behind me were laughing and joking and occasionally they touched my hair. I didn't know who they were. Then a young lady sat next to me. As far as I could tell she was dressed all in black, I turned around and asked her who she was and as she was telling me I saw eyes for the first time in eight years. I could not understand how this had happened. I thought that I had gained my sight back, but in reality she had very heavy eye shadow and her eyes were very black so I think that I was able to focus and in this way I saw her eyes. It was an extraordinary experience and I could not believe how clear this vision of this lady's eyes was.

She didn't stay very long, just enough time to say hello. She had quite an impact on me and I can honestly say that they were the only eyes that I had seen in eight years, highlighted by her heavy eye shadow which enabled me to see her eyes.

I made me consider going to my optician but he had told me that my eyes would not get any worse or any better so there was no point in me going anymore.

That was the end of that party and my unforgettable visionary experience.

At another garden party, I won the first prize. The lovely Administration Officer, who is very slim and cheerful, came running over the lawn to ask me to pull the next number out of the hat ready for the second prize. She then asked me what I wanted so I told her that I wouldn't have minded a bottle of white wine – a Chardonnay. She wasn't sure she had a bottle of white, but she ran back inside and did emerge with a bottle of Chardonnay. I thought to myself at that moment, how lucky I was to be in a home like Walstead, having people running back and forth to ensure that I am happy.

I challenge everyone to find a better home than this one. Walstead is a residential home, not a care home and offers superb facilities.

I do joke with the girls at meal times and they do laugh but not only with me. They just go around happily and never have any arguments unless the matron or deputy matron has to give somebody a little talk if they are not doing something right. Matron has to be firm and keep the staff in check but generally, the staff do their work diligently and always with joy and pleasure.

I have spoken about my home. I feel I have no other words to describe how wonderful it is. When I had been here for about a year we had a lot of ordinary people that came to stay with us as you do not have to qualify to live here, you can be in perfect health and come and live a life of luxury for as long as you please which is one of the reasons I chose this place.

I have the freedom to walk, I am not confined to a wheelchair because they let me use my zimmer frame and I can take as long as I want and I am never rushed. The deputy matron told me that she had only been here a couple of months before I arrived, but she is so good at what she does, it seemed she'd been here longer.

As I said, the first year we had many people coming in but after that we suddenly began to have important people arrive, for example, we had three ladies and by that I mean that they are titled ladies. We have various other people who have come here who are quite famous.

This is happening because this home has a very good reputation and people come here on recommendation. People outside are beginning to realise it and credit goes to matron and her staff for running the home so beautifully.

I am really grateful that I am so well looked after at Walstead Place. I am very happy here and have had the opportunity to meet many wonderful people. My daughter and son found this place for me. It was meant to be.

****

In my walk of life I have come to know a variety of personalities, and, as I sit in the warmth of my surroundings, I gather the thoughts and memories I treasure. I love to reflect upon situations and individuals who made me feel special. I have spoken at length about my wonderful family, but I have also made friends with some dear people that bring laughter and joy to me.

Roger and Eric are two wonderful people who have become dear and close friends. Two individuals with a wealth of knowledge and both with characters that reach out and embrace you and support you in a way that is very special to me.

I met Roger on a Wednesday when he came to introduce himself to me when I first moved into Walstead Place. I remember that day. He was smartly dressed and his movements were quick and agile for the plump little figure that leaned forward to shake my hand. A cuddly man I thought at the time.

We got talking and we exchanged brief histories of what and where we had been. I told him of my Wimbledon origins, Croydon and New Addington experiences, Crawley and a brief mention of a few other places. It emerged that his parents had owned a factory opposite where we lived in New Addington and that, if I looked out my window, I would have seen his parent's factory. In fact, he probably walked past my home each day on his way home from college. He told me that he and his parents would take walks in the woods not far from our house. It's quite incredible to meet someone years later and find out that you frequented or belonged to the same clubs. It turned out that Roger was also a member of Old Portlians Cycling Club, where I had been a member.

Roger and I have forged a friendship and he has helped me understand the foundations of my faith in God. I joined Bible classes which I found a bit complicated initially but Roger got me *The One Hundred Minute Bible* from which he reads to me each week and we discuss afterward. I do enjoy listening to him read because he reads with a passion and determination that heightens my own enthusiasm for the good message the bible delivers.

Roger doesn't talk much about himself, but I believe he is an important man in his own right. Coincidently, he studied and qualified as a professional accountant in ACWA. He didn't get to use his qualification and chose to turn his attentions to theology and the church where he felt enriched and fulfilled. He tells me one of the stories of how he became immersed and committed to delivering the word of God.

He was not home at the time when his wife had received a phone call from someone wanting to reach him. They hadn't left a forwarding number and rang off saying they'd call again. When the caller eventually called back, he asked Roger if he would travel to Cardiff, expenses paid, to deliver a speech to a congregation about an aspect of the Bible. Roger obliged and I guess this was part of his journey towards what he does and stands for today.

Roger is a blessed and wonderful man. He is never boastful. He is deeply committed to his cause. I have benefited so much from sharing his knowledge. This is my one friend who stands as a pillar amongst men and women. A man of depth and warmth who shares effortlessly and wants for nothing but to spread goodwill and the word of God. This is what Jim Parker aspired to from the day my mother told me about Jesus and today I have someone with whom I can share my own aspirations, for we have an understanding of what gives us joy.

****

Let me tell you about Eric, my other dear, dear friend, who is such a pillar of strength. He makes me laugh so much; I'd fall over if I didn't have my walking stick. This dear friend fills my heart and days with the kind of laughter and joy hard to describe. I would need to write a separate book on the things we've done together in the short time I have known him.

Eric is as robust in character as he is in physical attribute. A man of honour and with a big hearty voice I've had pleasure to chorus with during our moments of song and trips down memory lane. When he talks or sings his voice wraps round you like the embrace of a warm cuddly blanket. What strength one draws from this presence of sturdy, uncompromised stature. I do feel loved and appreciated when I am with him and as safe as houses. Eric is my taxi driver and my beloved friend.

Eric has a daughter Nina. She is a lovely lady and has a big and beautiful home which she keeps so spotlessly clean. Nina is married to Mo who also drives me around if Eric is unable to pick me up. Eric looked after Nina on his own from when she was two years old. That can't have been easy, but he did a great job, because Nina is a good and stable lady, and her husband Mo is as funny and witty as his father-in-law Eric. Nina is also a great cook. She often sends me the most wonderful strawberry treats with Eric. As I mentioned before, food is one of my passions and I have always been lucky to have these wonderful ladies that send me samples of their pastries, cookies and all sorts of wonderful edible delights.

Eric and I spend quite a bit of time together and he always has a funny trick up his sleeve to show me. My favourite is when he does his impressions of famous personalities especially Roy Fox, Geraldo or Billy Cotton. He really gets into character and does a good old impression that leaves me in fits of laughter. These moments I spend with Eric are so precious and I hope that others can be as fulfilled in friendship as I am when I'm with Eric. I know he will do anything to protect and look after me.

Even our trips to Bournemouth in his beautiful Mercedes are filled with joy and laughter. Never a dull moment with Eric, a truly remarkable, genuine man.

I am happy for Eric that his blessings are his wonderful daughter and son-in-law Mo. Mo and Nina are two dependable and responsible individuals and when Eric decides to retire, I believe they will take over the taxi business.

I forgot to mention that Eric also has three wonderful grandchildren, Adam, Laura and the youngest Joseph who is only fifteen years old. They also have a wispy little dog called Marlow who gets up to all sorts of mischief when he's out with Joseph. I've met Marlow and he is such a clever little dog that it brings back memories of my own dog Trixie. Whenever I see Marlow, he goes potty and jumps up to greet me when I wind my window down. Eric always says "Give Jim a kiss, Marlow" and he comes forward to lick me …

Aawwh he is so lovely. Sometimes Marlow will jump in the car and come and lie across my legs, but then Eric will tell him to excuse himself, so Marlow will look up at me, give me a lick then move and sit beside me. Such a clever little thing. I believe Joseph is teaching Marlow to count. So far he can count to three. If you count one, he barks once….. then you count two, he barks twice, then three and he barks three times. It's so hilarious and wonderful how they understand instructions.

It's really refreshing knowing that Eric is so reliable. He is patient and caring and never fazed about taking me anywhere. We go shopping together to Sainsbury's and even there Eric is popular and known by the staff. When we arrive at the parking lot, there's a young lad who will especially run and fetch a wheelchair to assist me when he sees Eric pull up.

I am really well looked after and glad to have someone there for me. Of course, his job is driving taxis, but Eric is more than a taxi driver for me. Eric provides me with the comfort and security of knowing that he is there for me firstly in the capacity of friend. He does things for me that no ordinary taxi driver would. As a taxi driver, I would say that he deserves an award because he's an excellent driver and such is the comfort of his car, I have never experienced backache even when we go away on long journeys.

Friendship is a responsibility not an opportunity, and I have a friend who has taken me under his wing and looks out for my well-being. I am very protective over my friends and those who are there for me. I am truly grateful to have forged this wonderful friendship with Eric. God bless this dear friend and his family.

****

Finally, I must share my last story with you all of a great moment of encouragement and enthusiasm. Quite recently our new entertainment manager, a lovely talented young lady came with her mum and dad to entertain us at the home. Her dad has a wonderful deep voice and her mum plays the piano beautifully. They heard that I was writing my book and they bought me a tape recorder with a built in microphone to encourage me to take my project forward. I was very touched by this gesture and here I say over and over again that there are people out there willing to give so much to others and we need to learn from these instances that life is not about material wealth. The gifts of unity and kindness are by far the greatest of all things to give.

It takes great character to do the things our entertainment manager does. Of course, we can argue that it's her job – but be aware that not just anyone can do any job. Certain jobs require certain strengths, skills and personality. Don't think that I'm a romantic, over-generous with praise. With age comes wisdom and I have come to appreciate the greatness of others and see how hard some work to do things that bring joy and unity if only for a moment.

Walstead Place has a wealth of talent and the activities organised by the staff offers great encouragement to its residents. Whilst the bingo, board games, knitting sessions or outings would bring tears to the average Joe, they do mean a great deal to the elderly. The talent and choice of staff required to sustain a high standard to ensure the elderly are well cared for is fundamental and key to the running a successful organisation.

9

FINAL THOUGHTS

I close my book with the knowledge that I have come to terms with my trials and tribulations and now I surround myself with people who bring meaning and joy to my life. I encourage you all to do the same. Don't wait to be old to have good friends; don't wait to be older to do good deeds. For those of you who have talent and I am sure all of you do, I encourage you to reach out and make a difference. Judge not lest ye be judged, but do appreciate and fill your coffers, not with worldly wealth but with wholesome ideals that will render you better people. This will prepare you for the moments when you are least strong and attract the good to reach out and lend that helping hand.

Now all that is left for me to do is to finalise my business with the Imperial War Museum to ensure that my awards and my history are rightfully recorded. At the time when the early whisper of war set tongues into wagging frenzy, I proudly volunteered to honour my country, but was dashed when it had become clear that Churchill put victory above life. It had been a hard fact to swallow, but I live to tell the story and hope at least now my contribution will be appreciated.

It is 6th August 2008 and I have just had some very important news about the Atlantic Star which I received. I believe that I am the only ordinary airman to have been awarded this star of which I am very proud. The government states army and navy personnel may get this medal, but they do not mention that an ordinary airman can get it, which is why I am absolutely convinced that I am probably the only airman to receive that service medal. When you go to a war zone you get a star and I have three of them in order: the Atlantic Star, the African Star and the Italian Star, which were three different war campaigns.

I am going to visit the Imperial War museum in the near future to find out if I am actually listed as being awarded the Atlantic Star. If not, I want to know why. There is the history of all our boys involved with our troops at home and abroad who served the King and then our Queen.

My decision to write my book *Just an Ordinary Man* has given me great pleasure and I am glad to be able to share my story. I hope to have enlightened readers and I bid you all goodwill and peace, and thank you for reading my story.

The End!